Mandala

Coloring Book for Adults

72 Stress Relieving Mandalas

Printed in the United States of America

ISBN: 978-1-63540-004-5

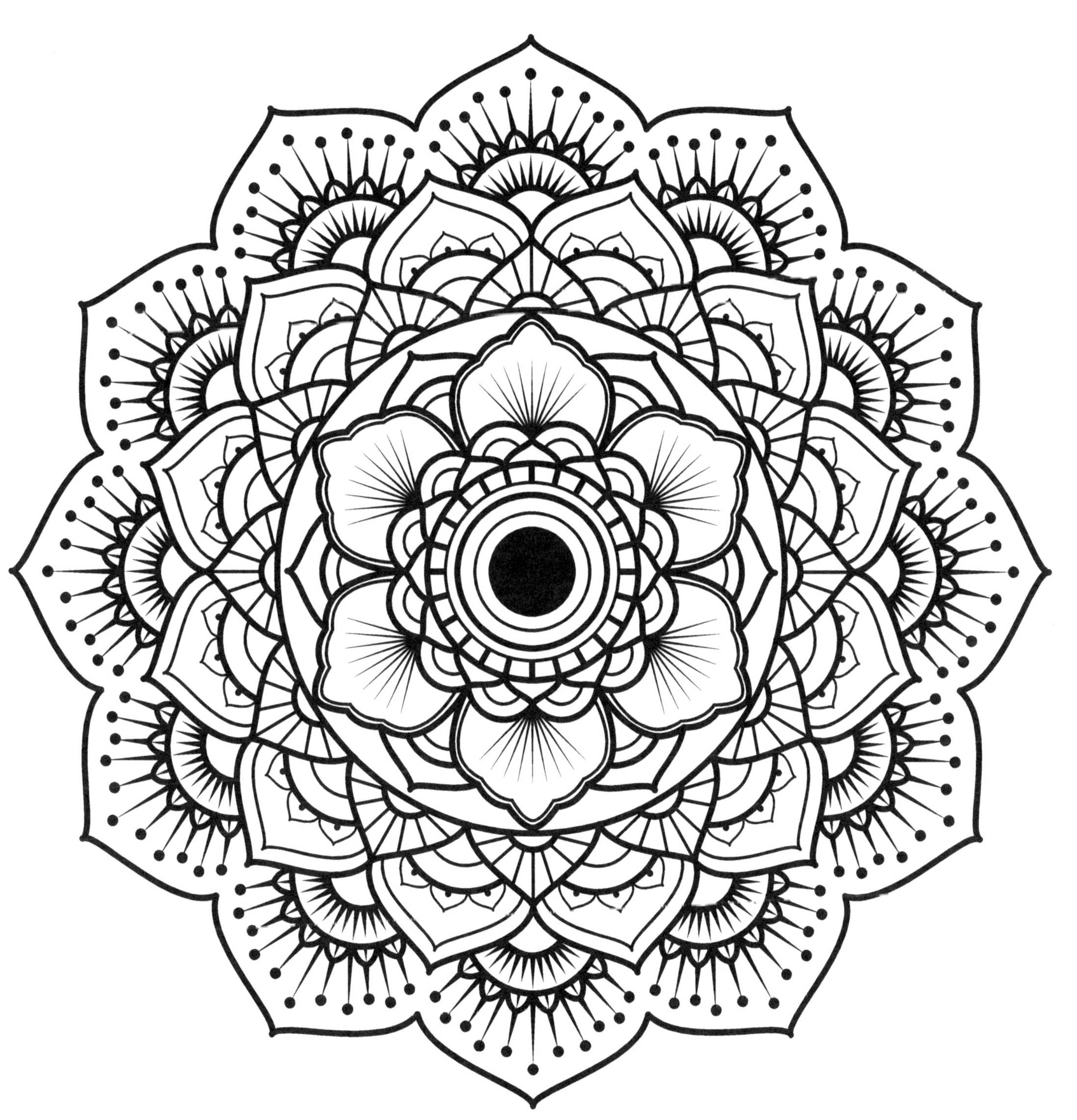

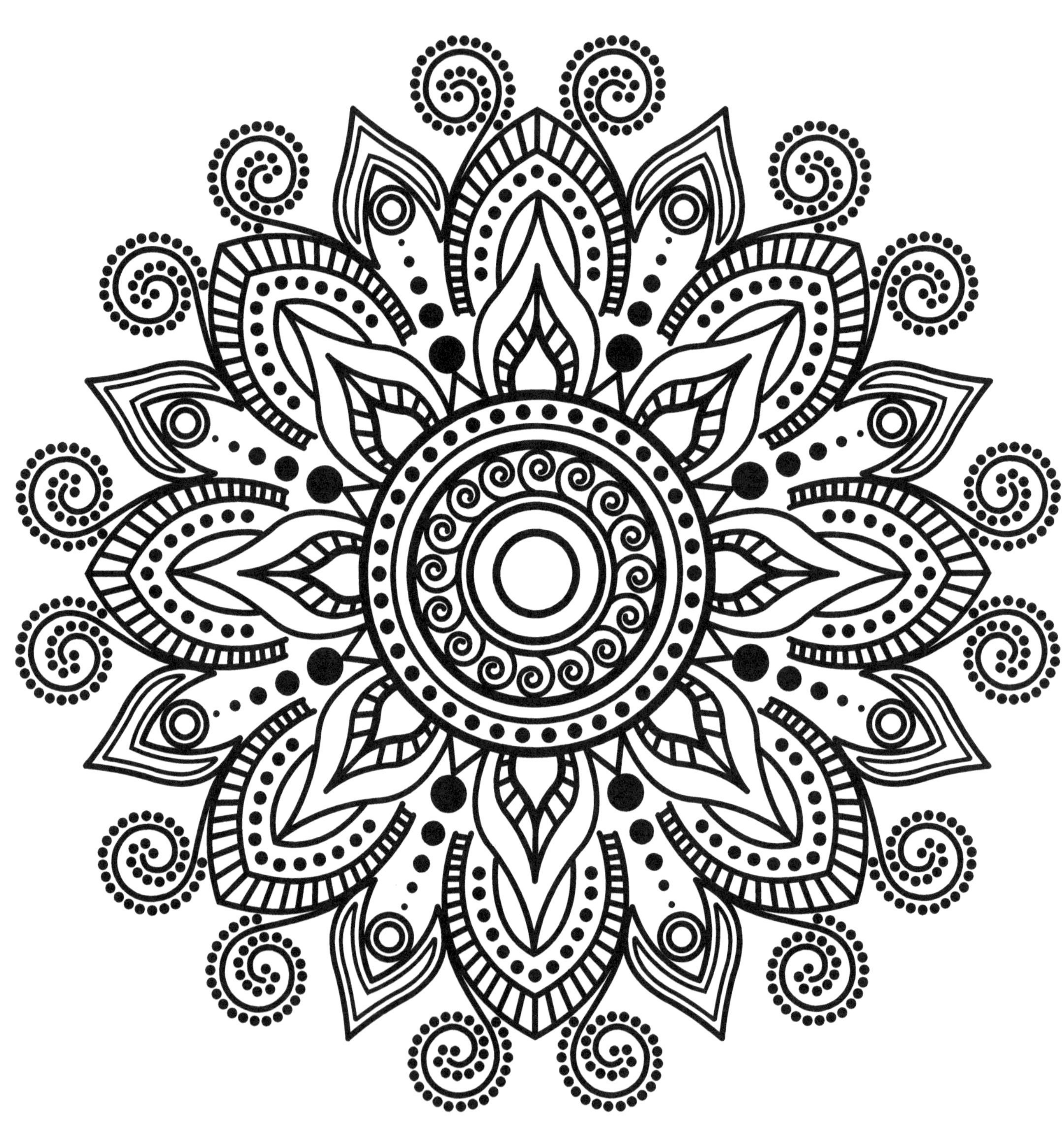

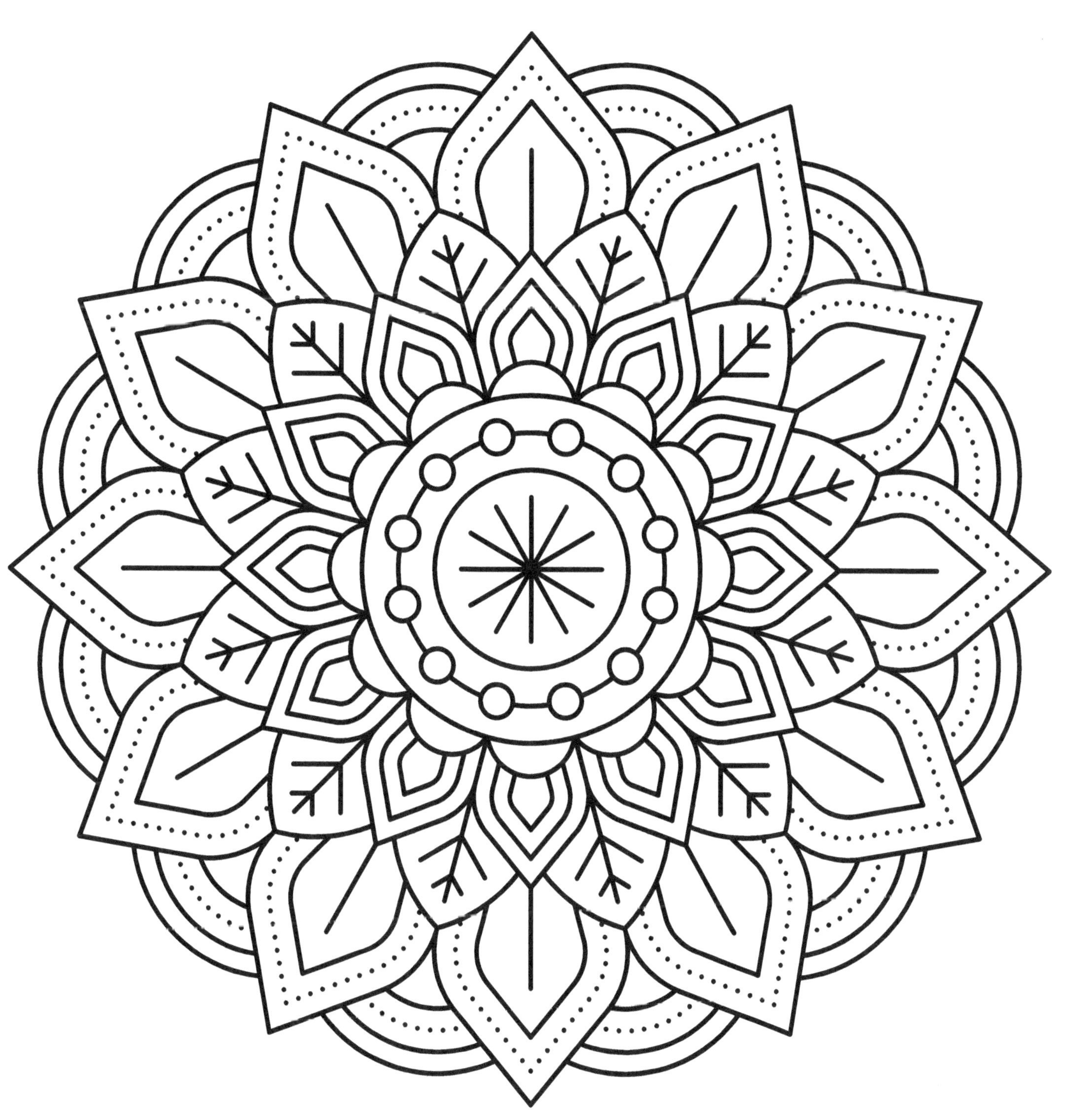

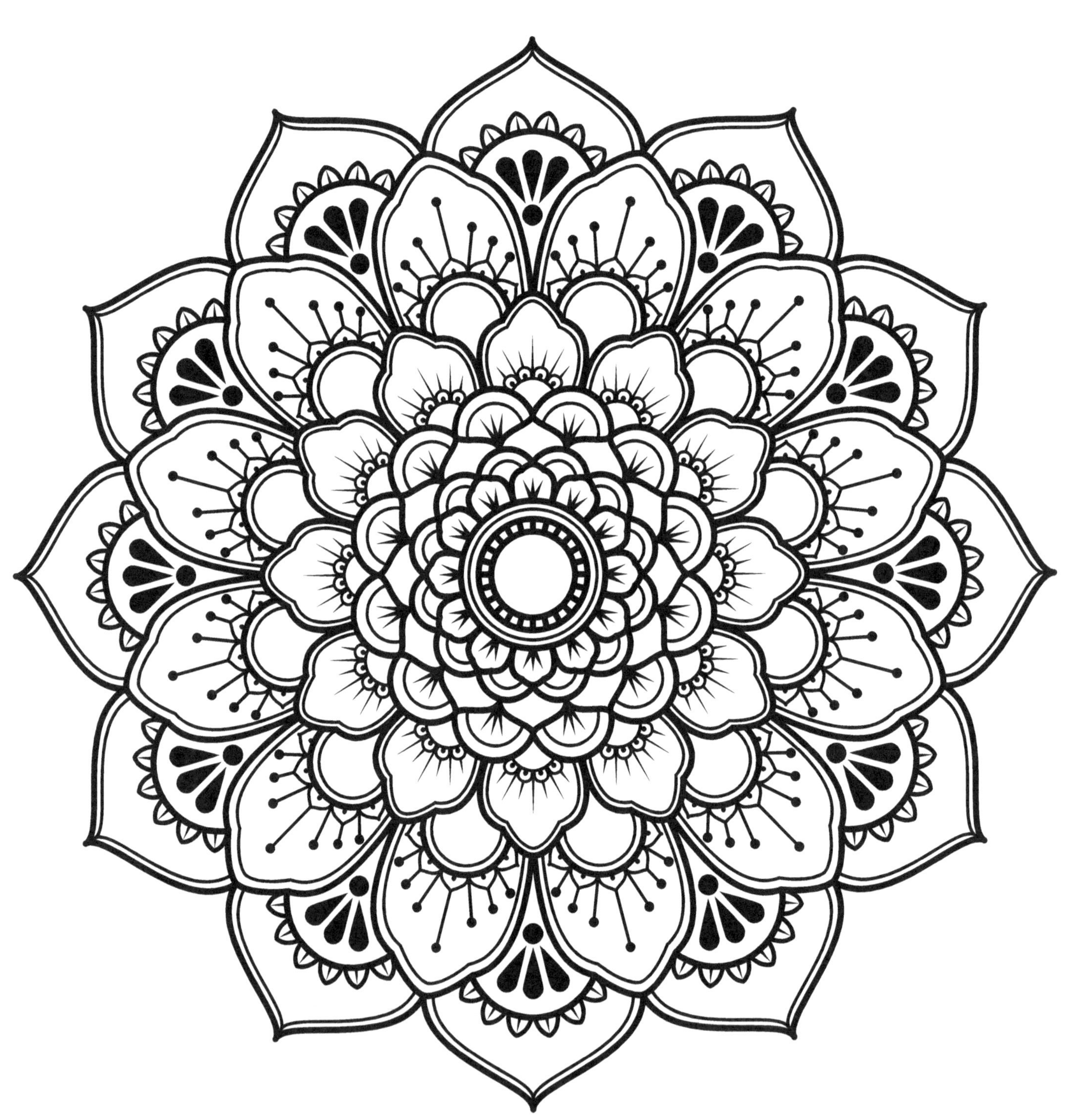

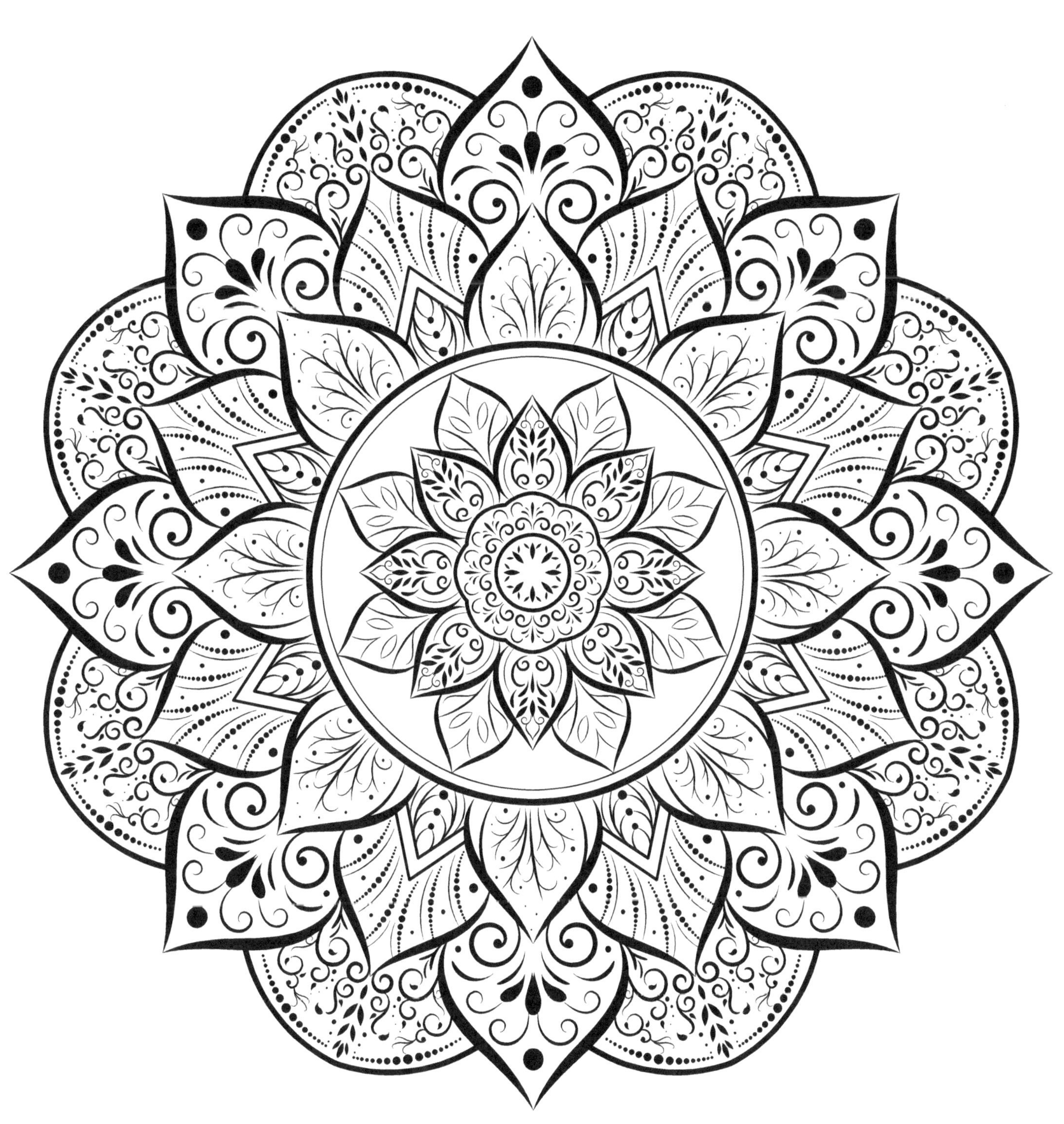

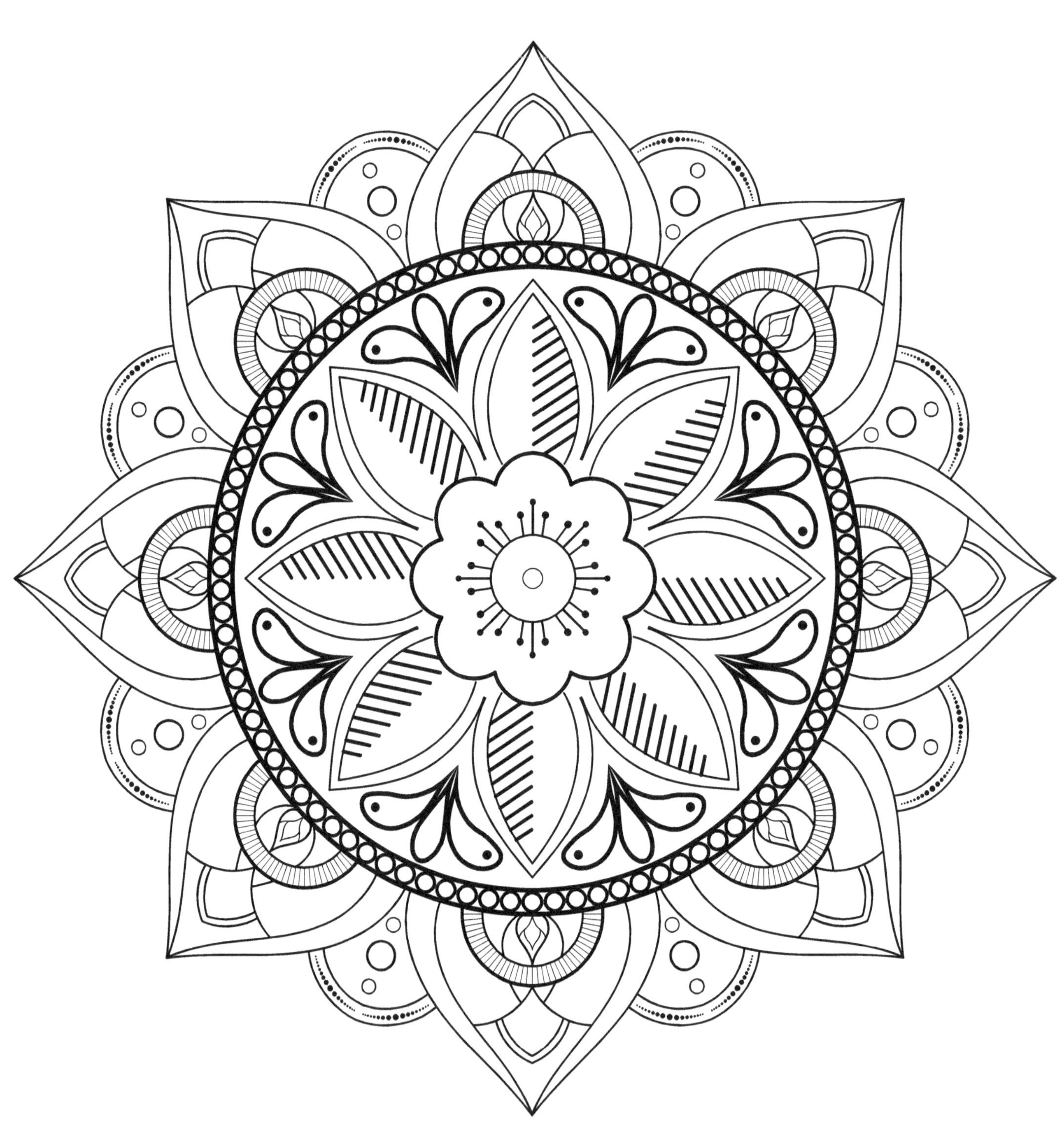

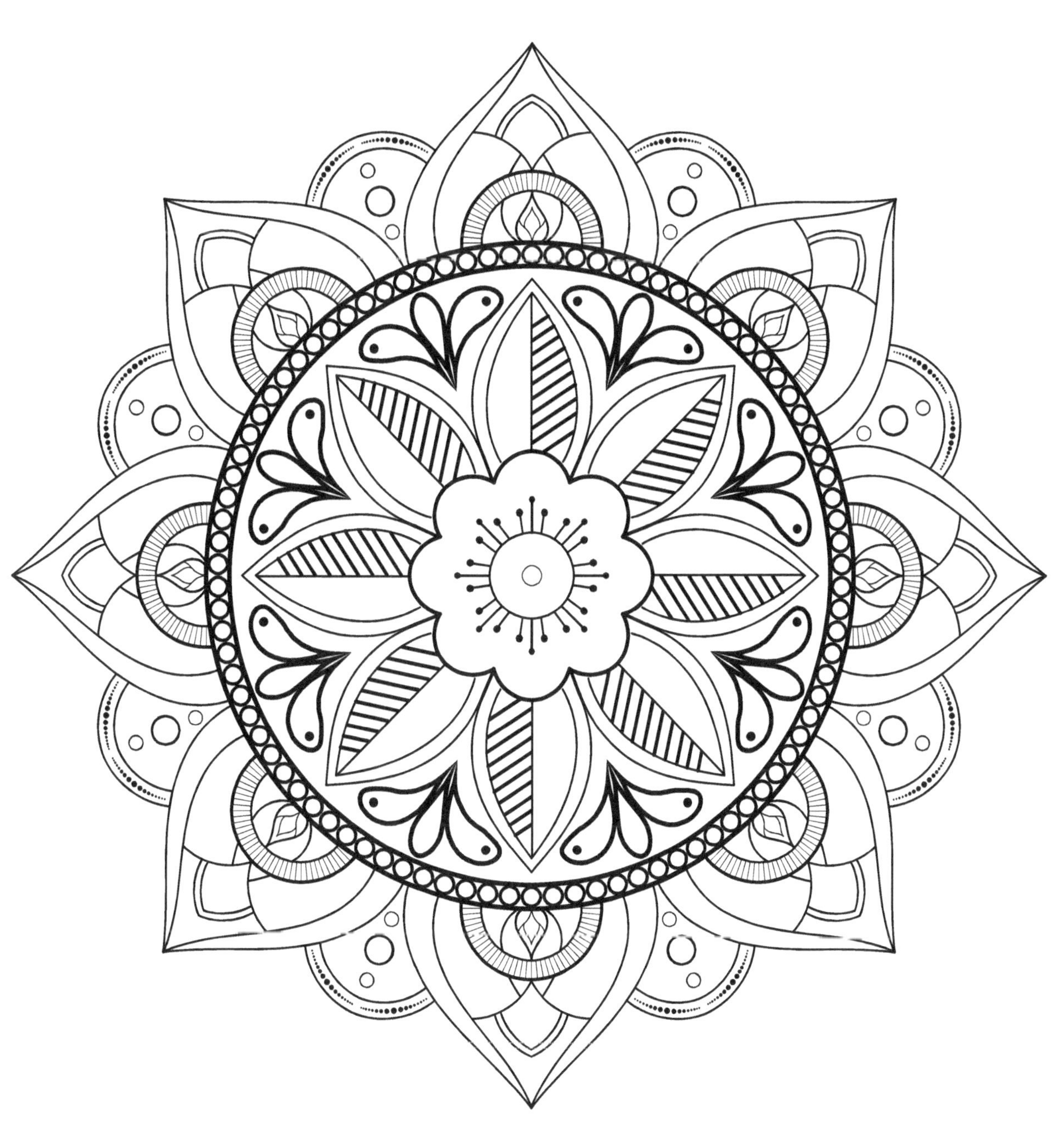

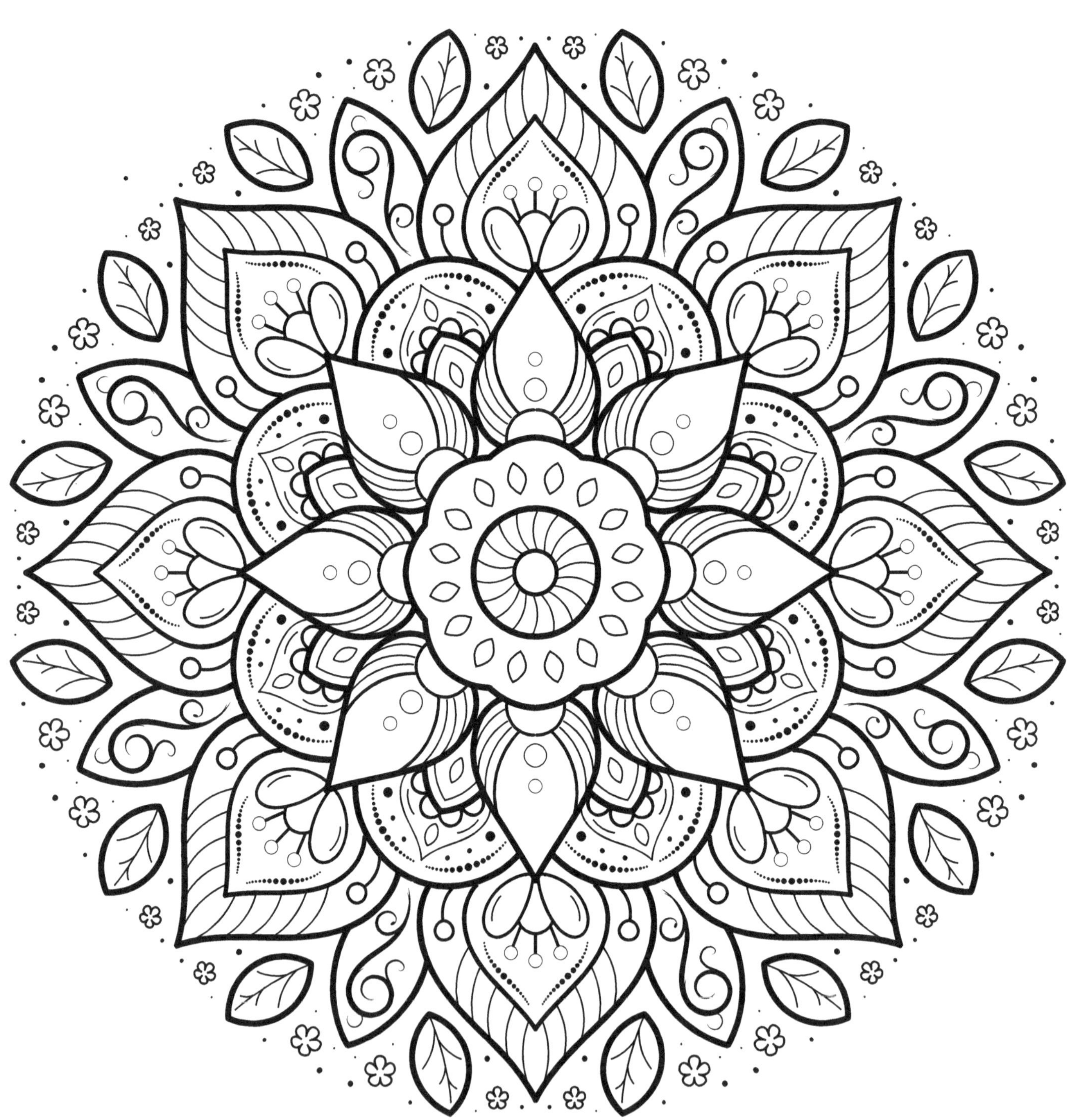

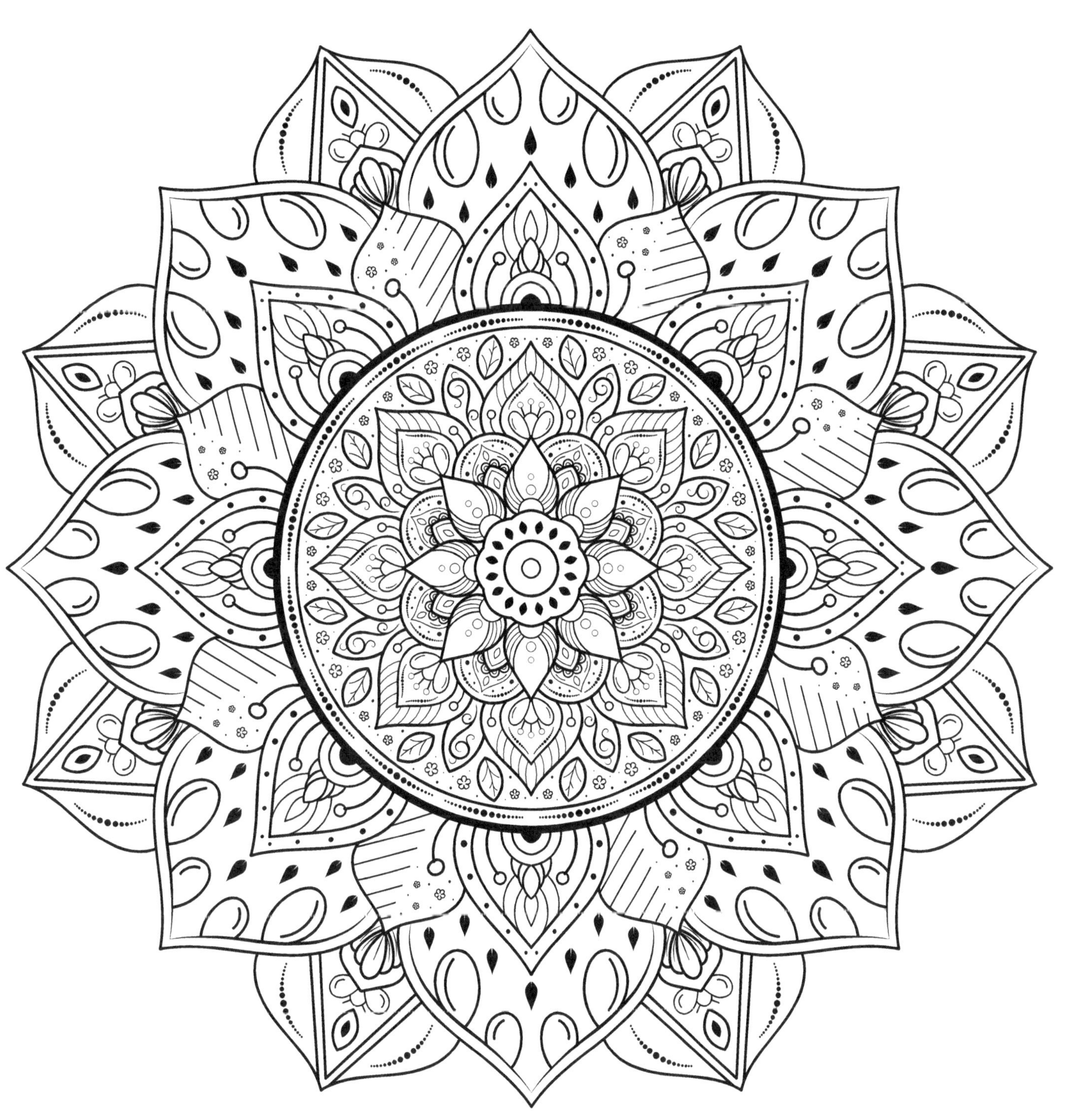

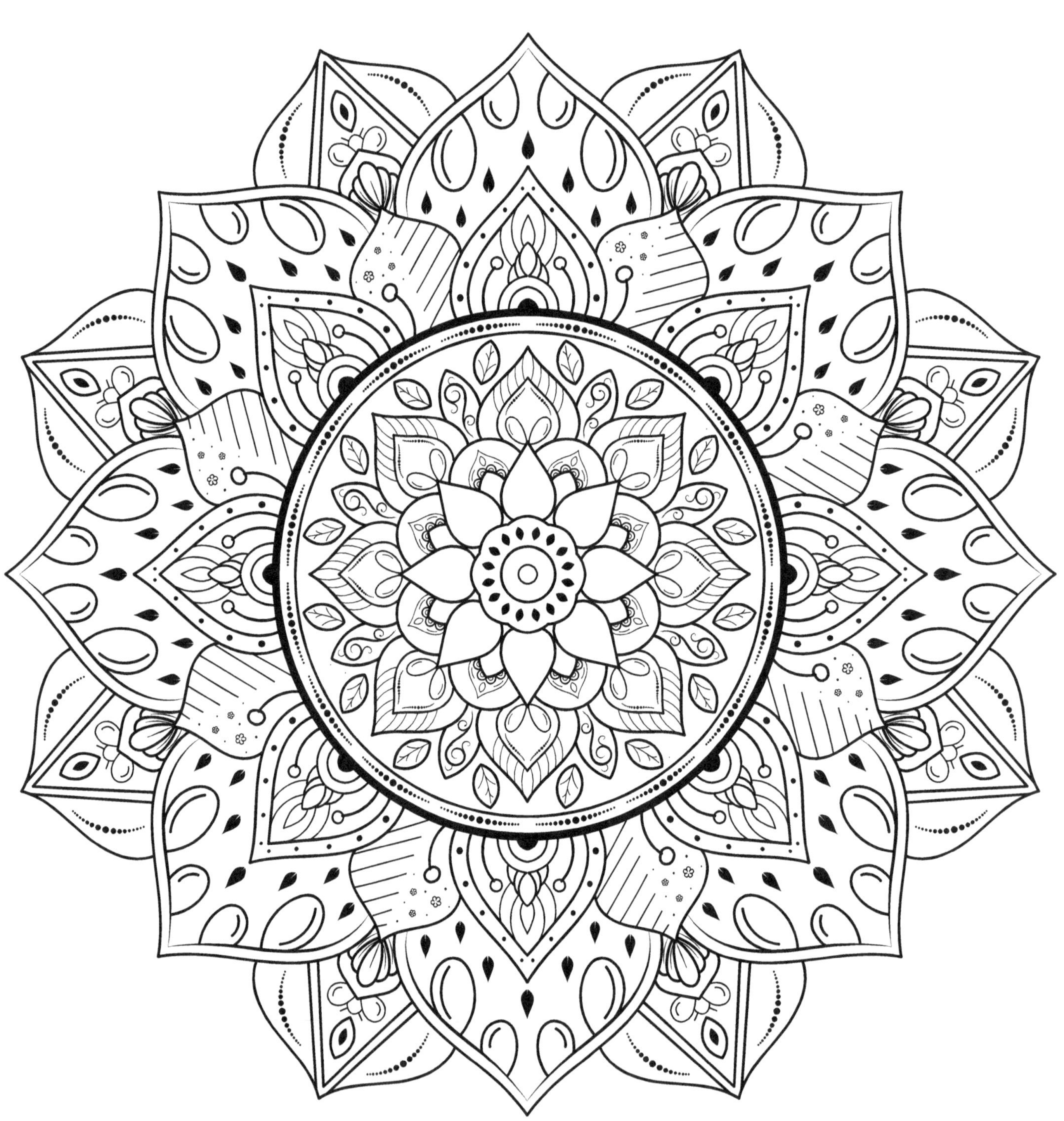

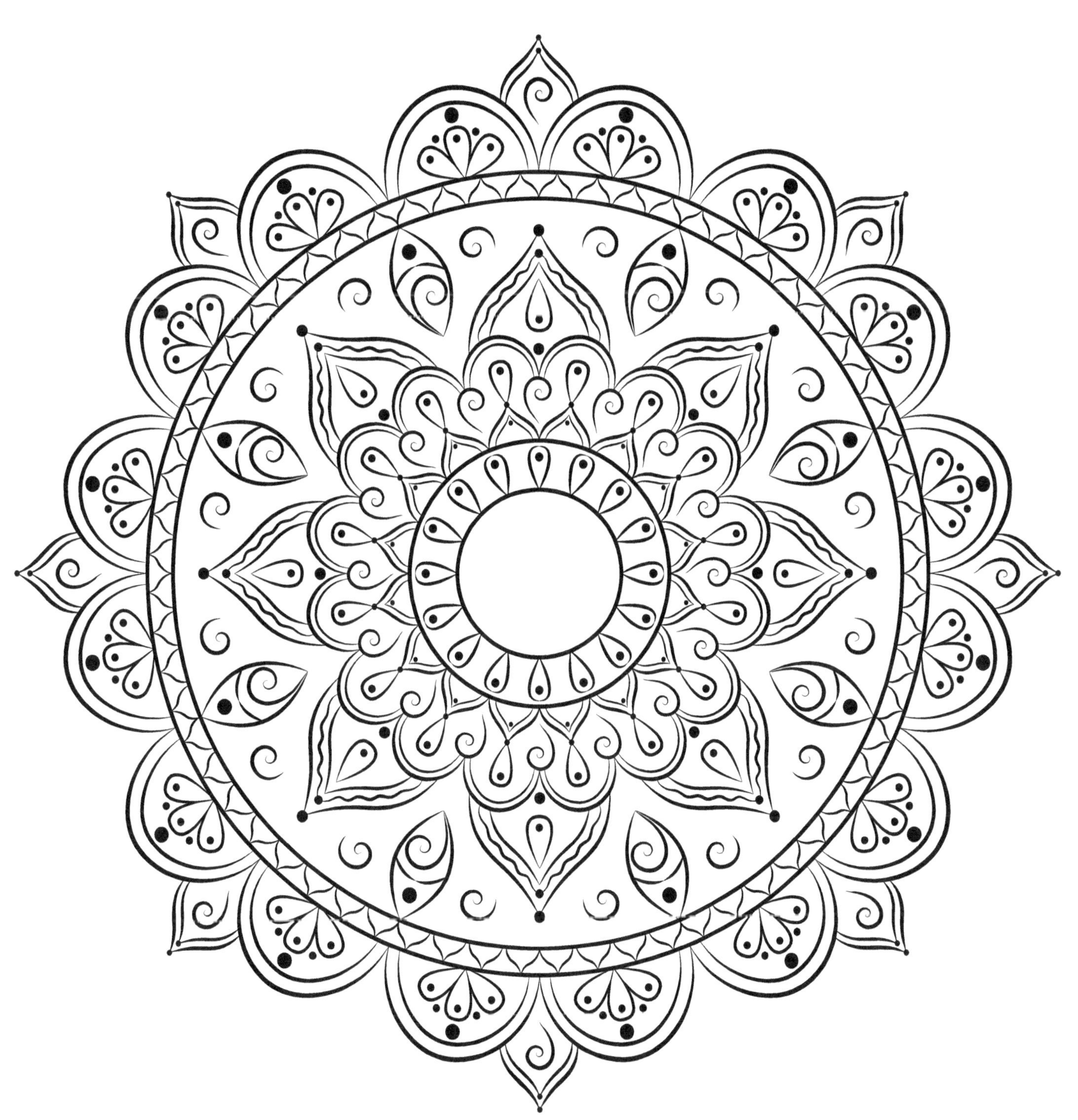

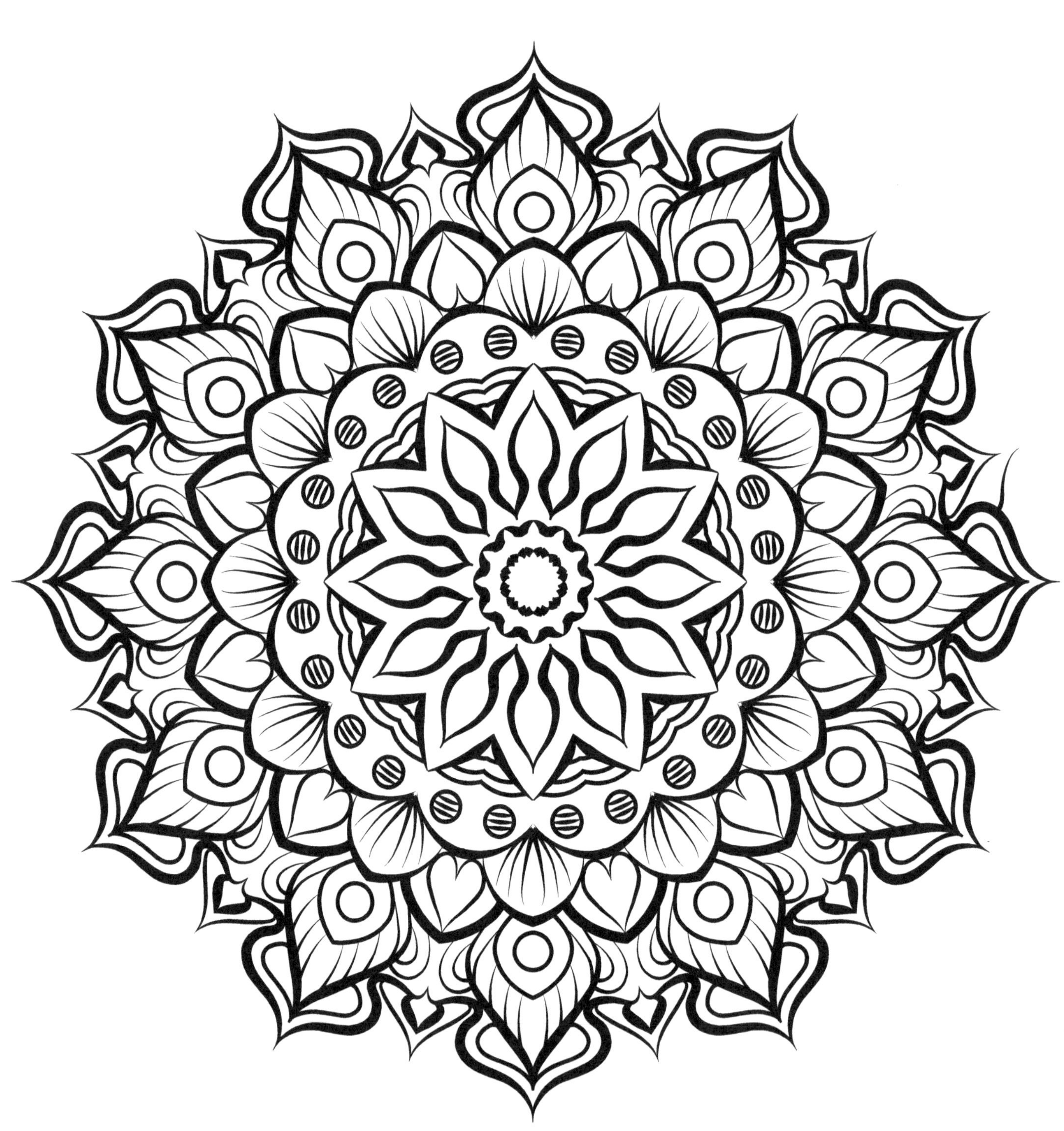

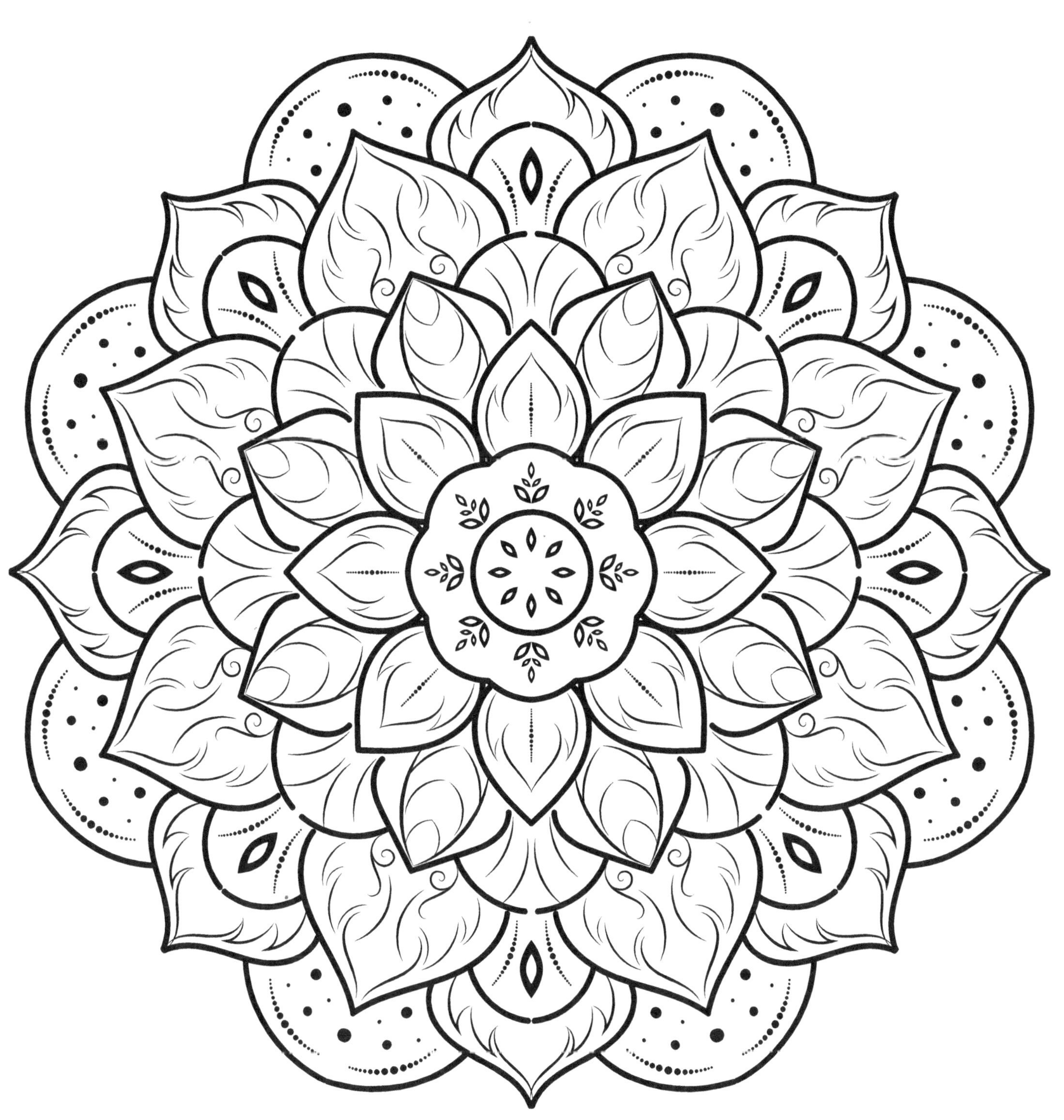

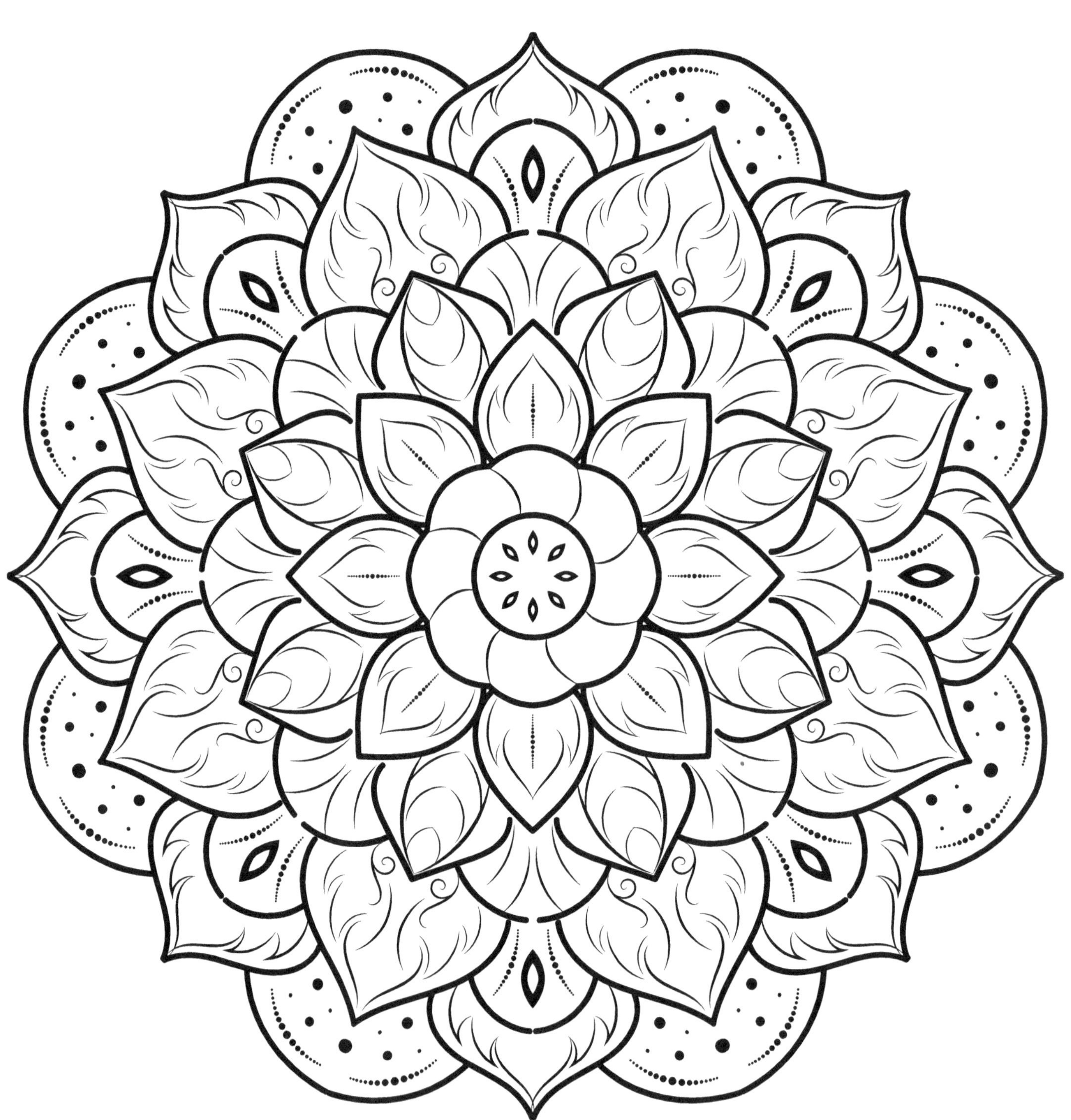

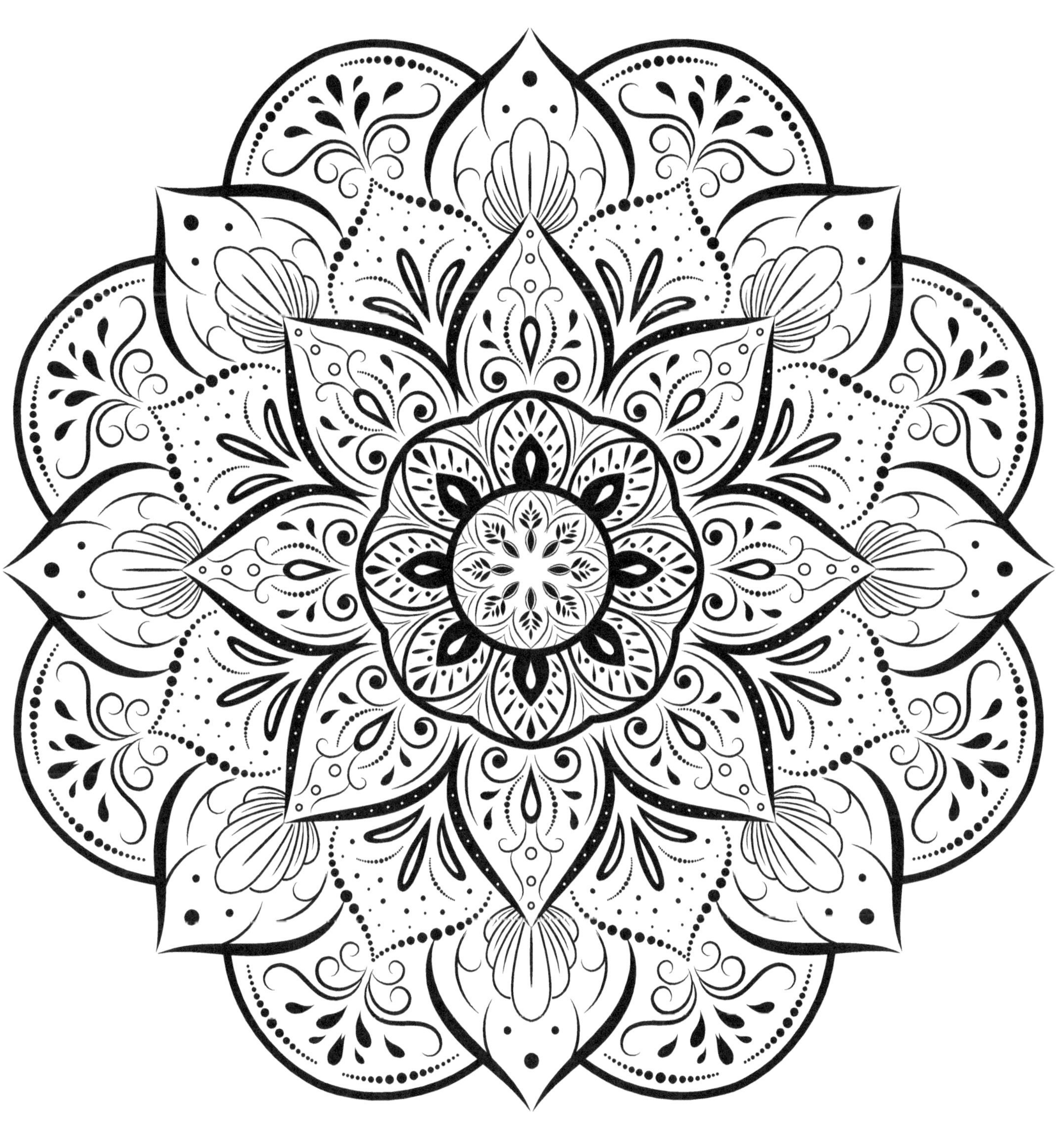

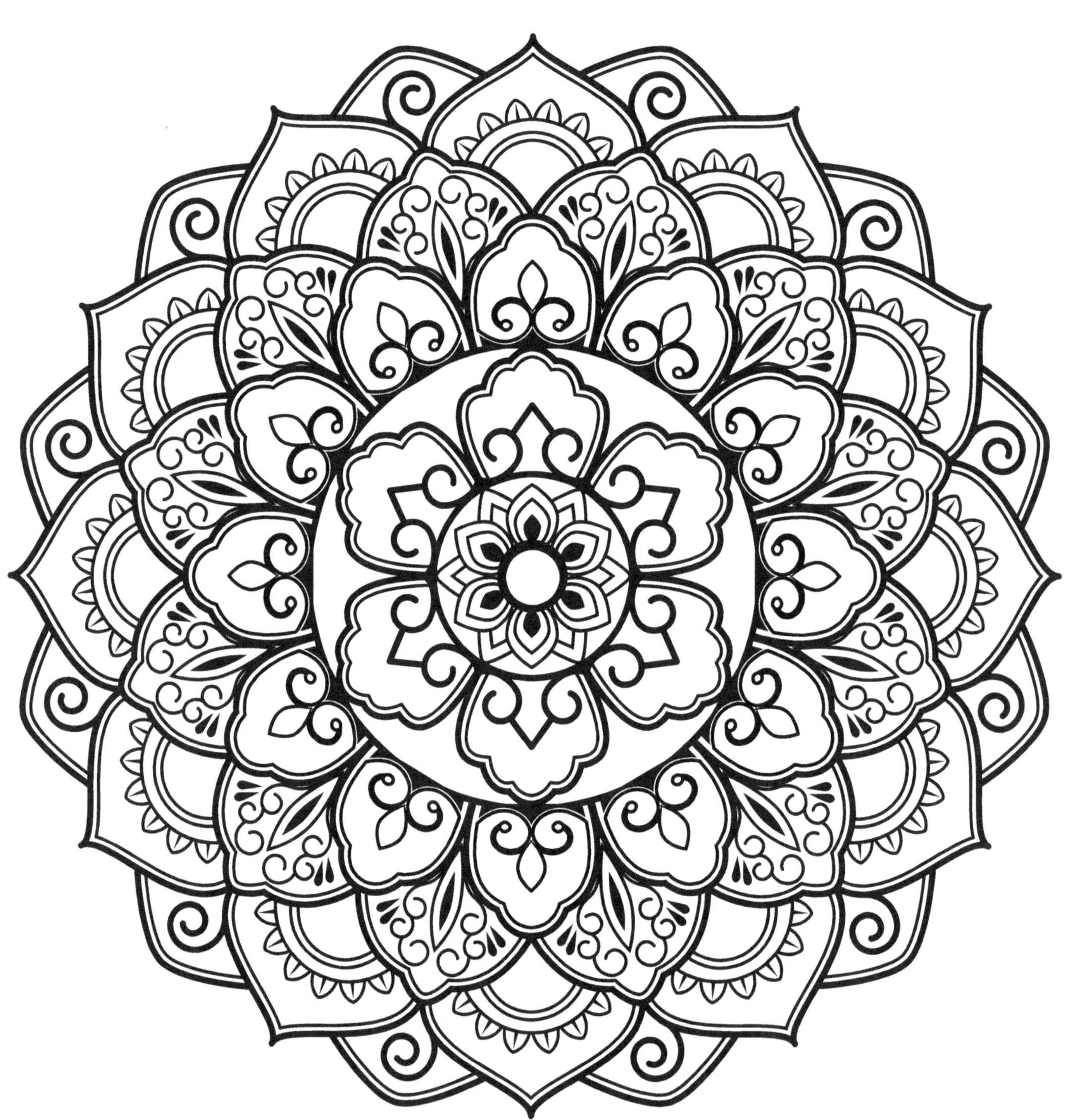

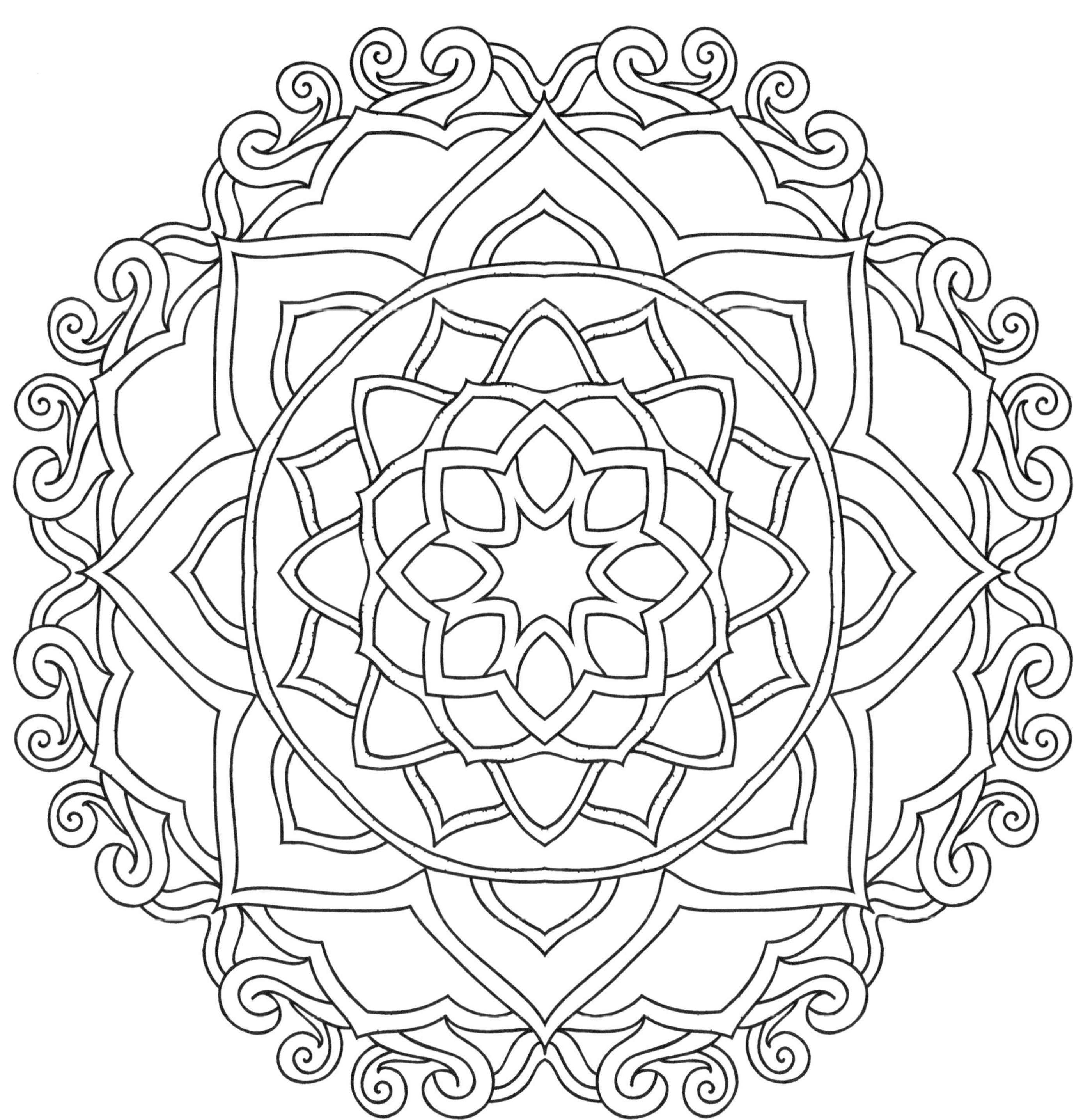

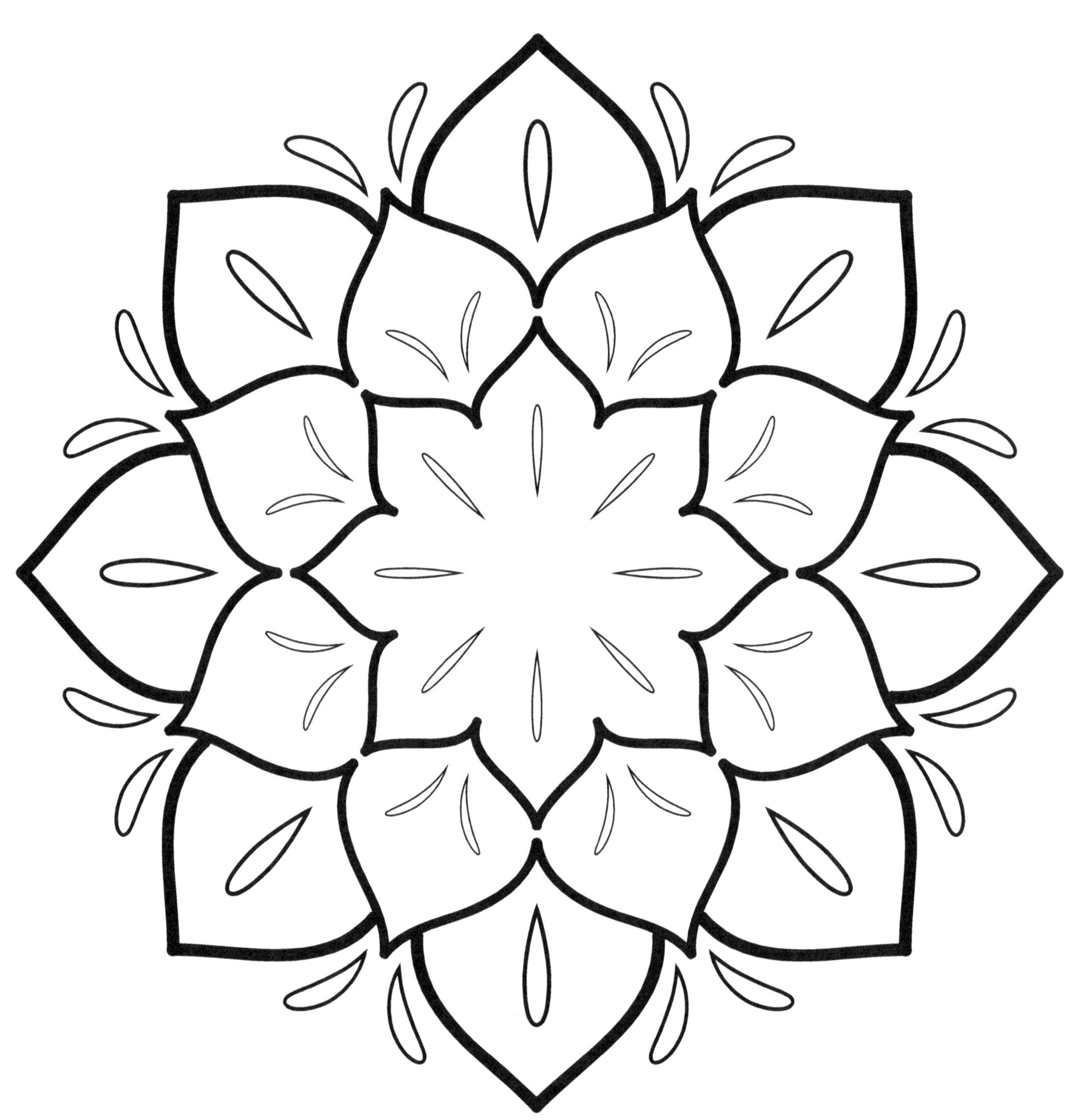

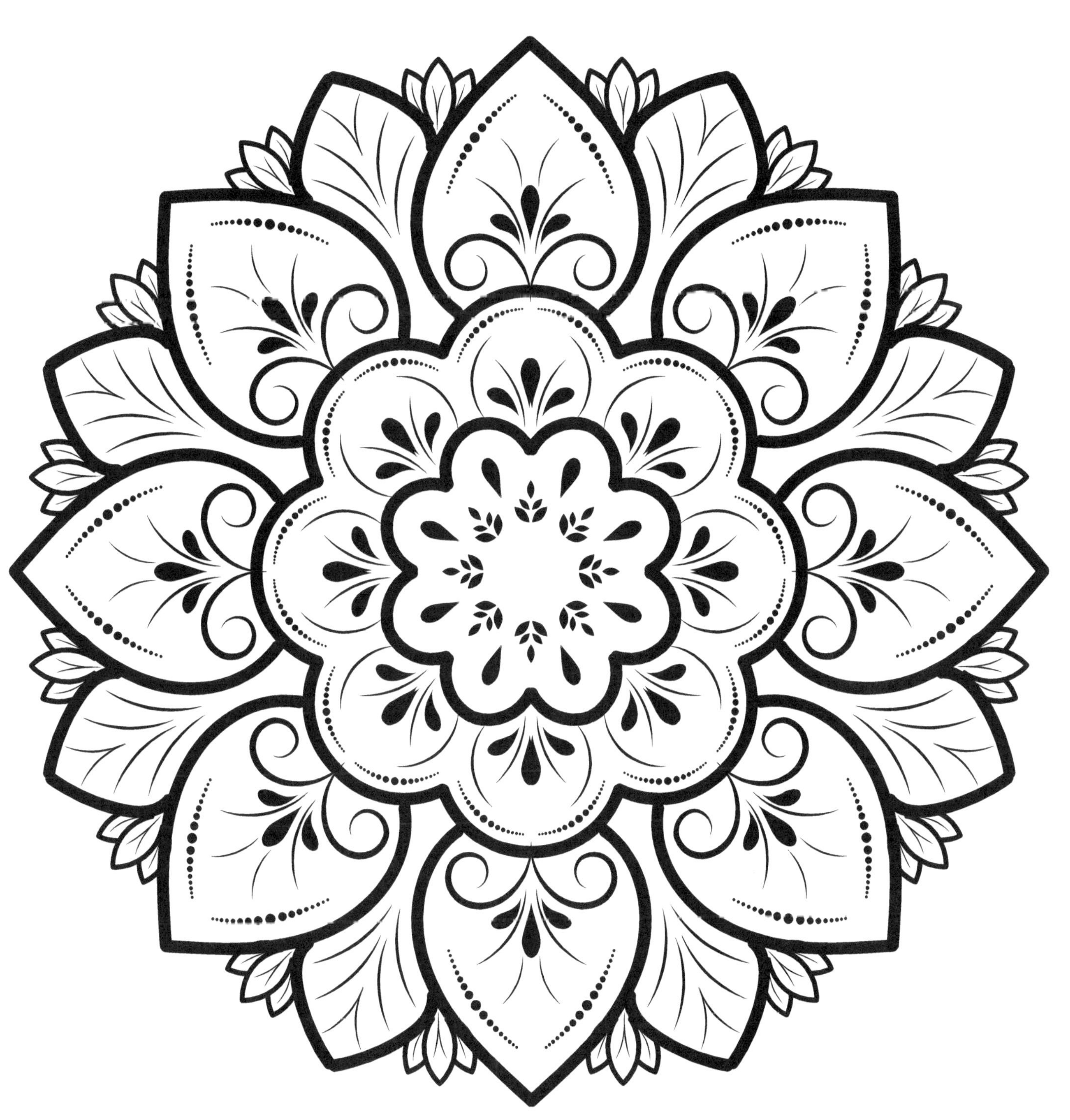

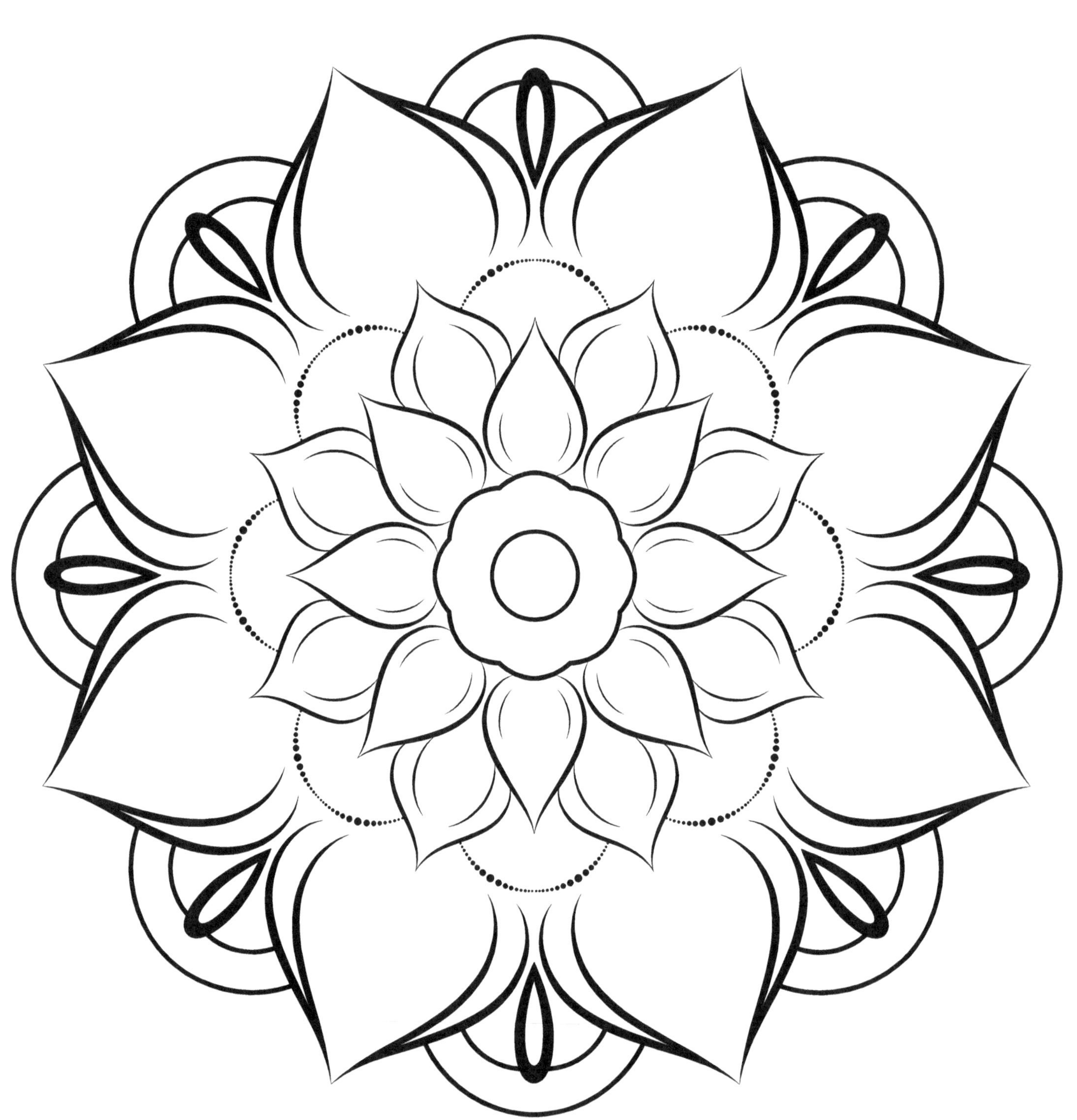

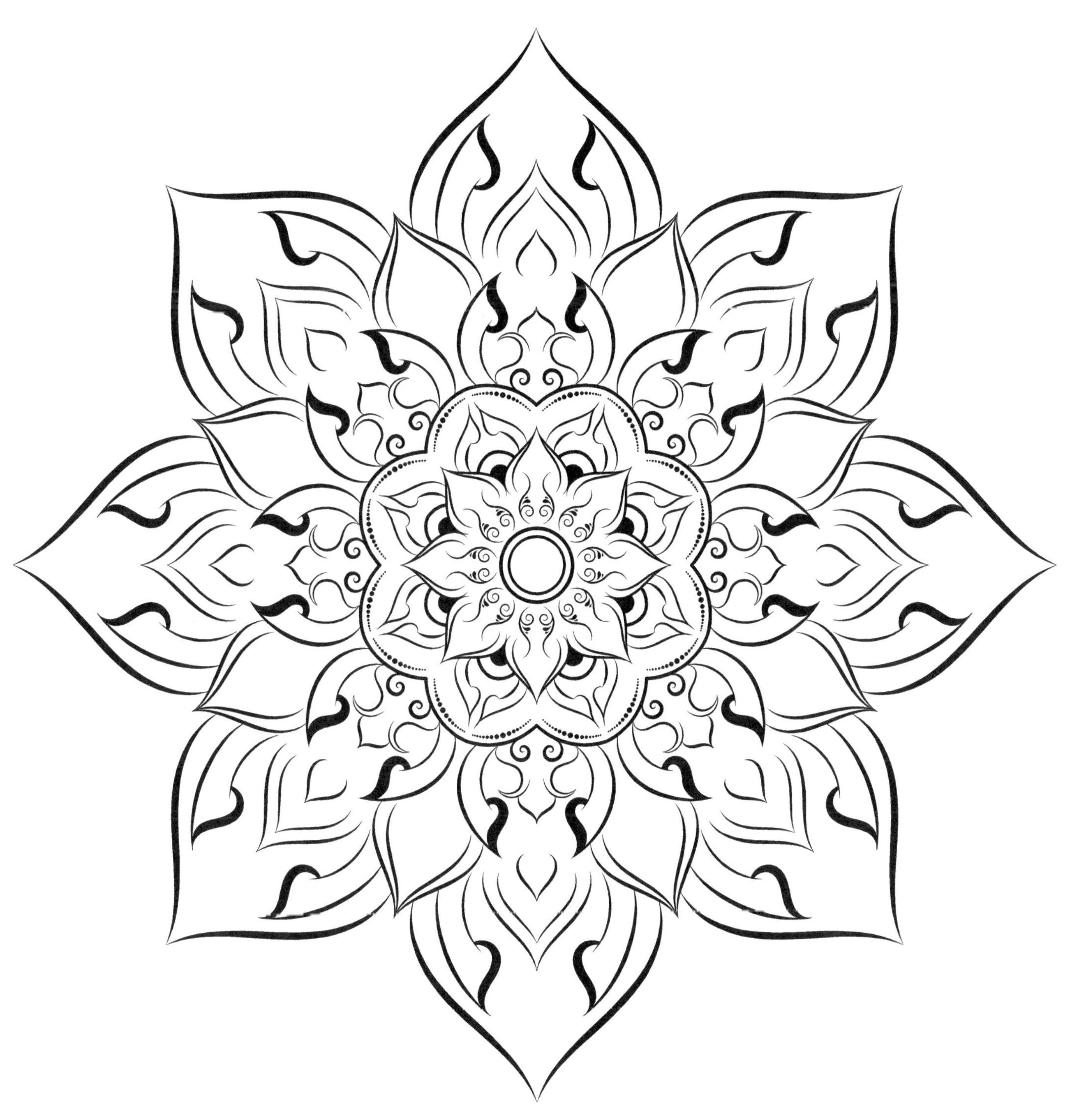

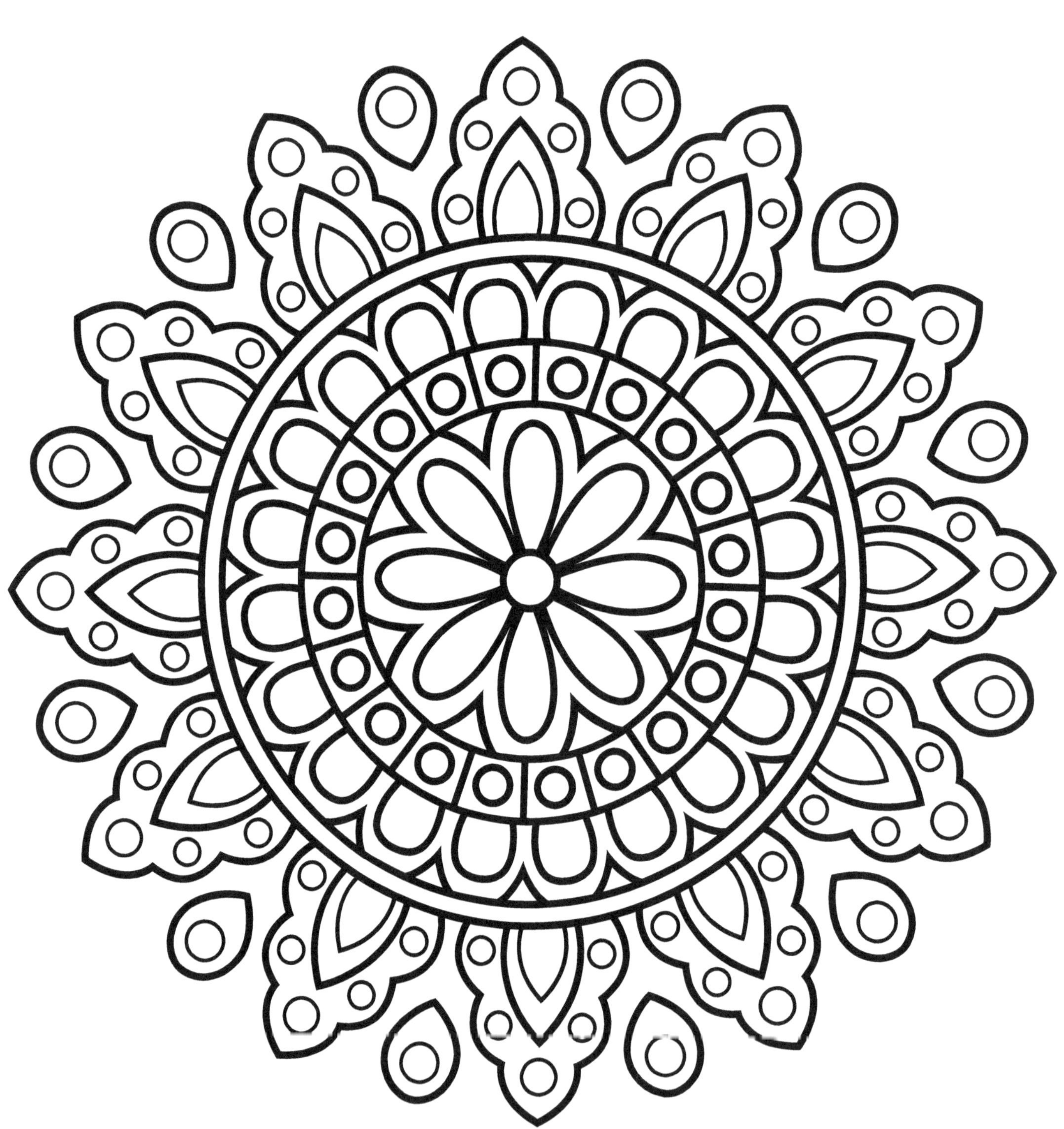

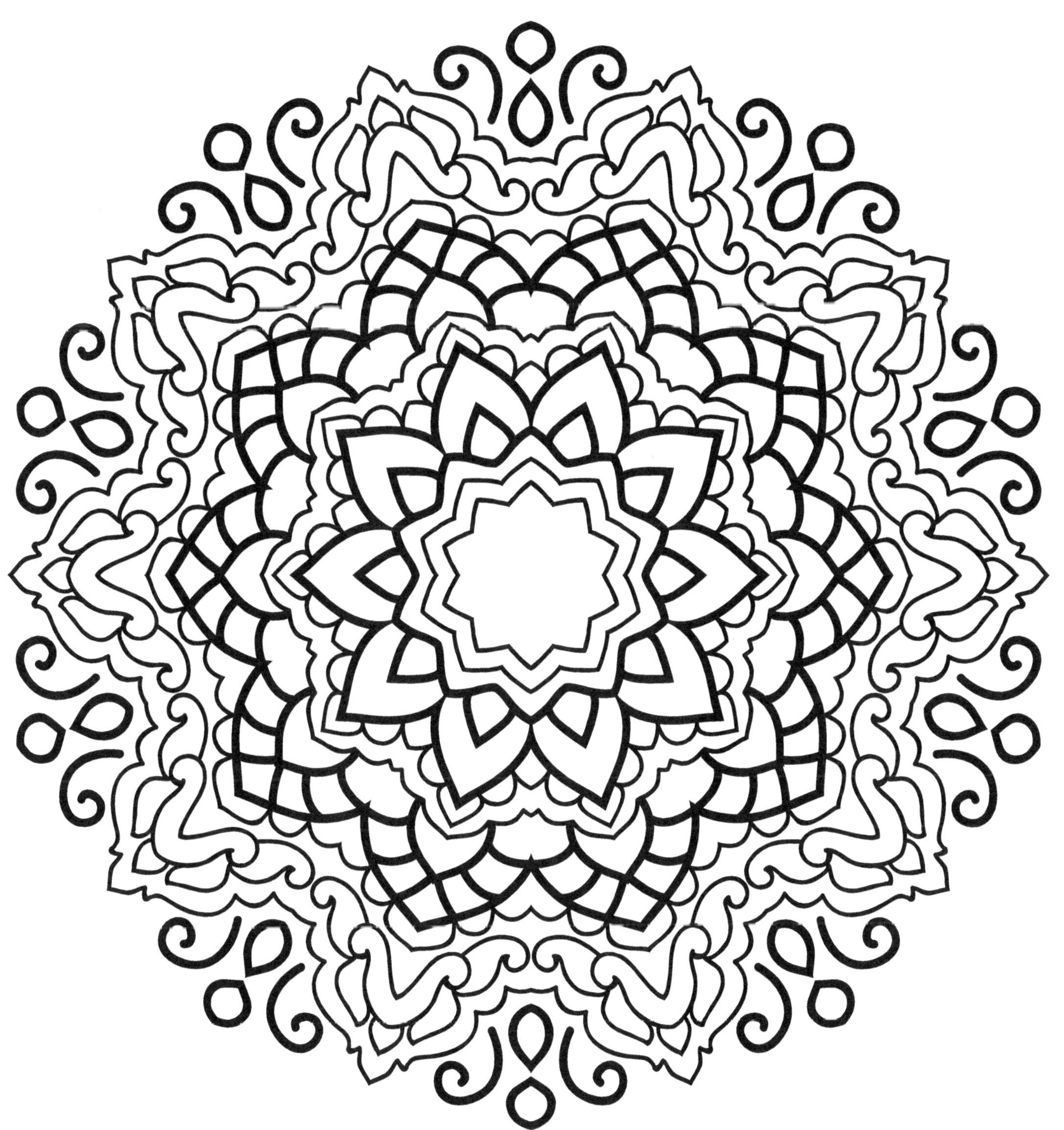

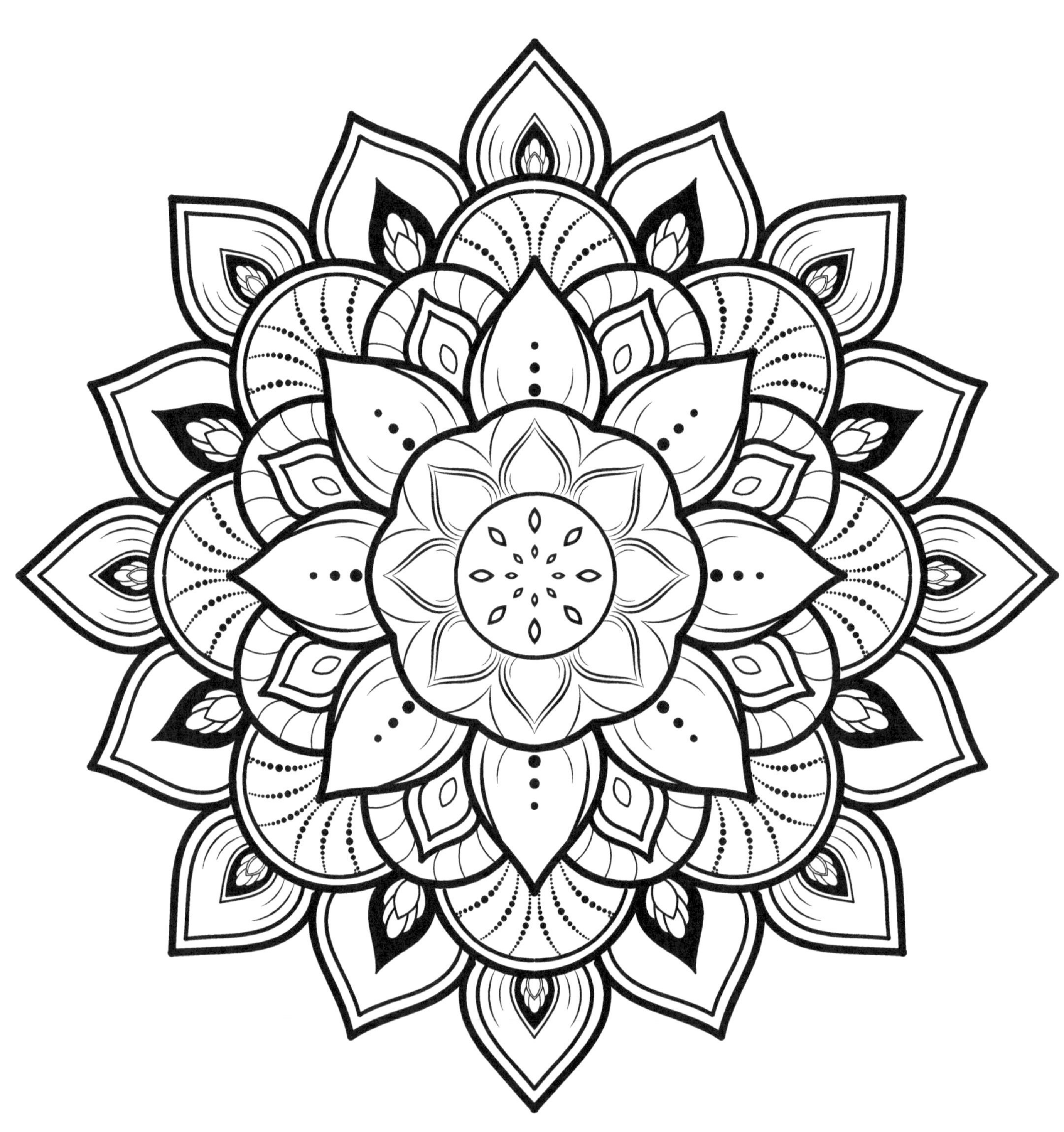

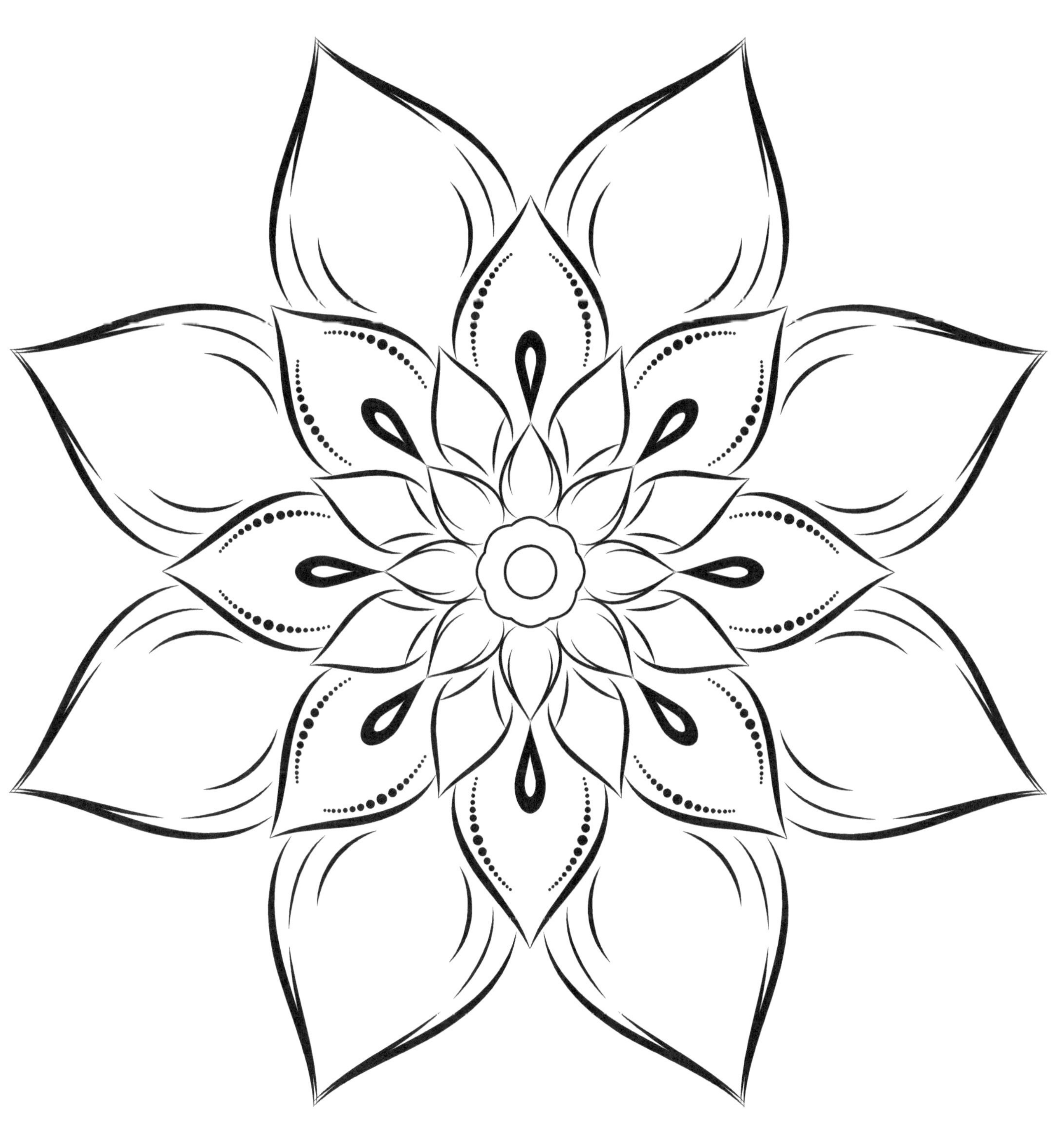

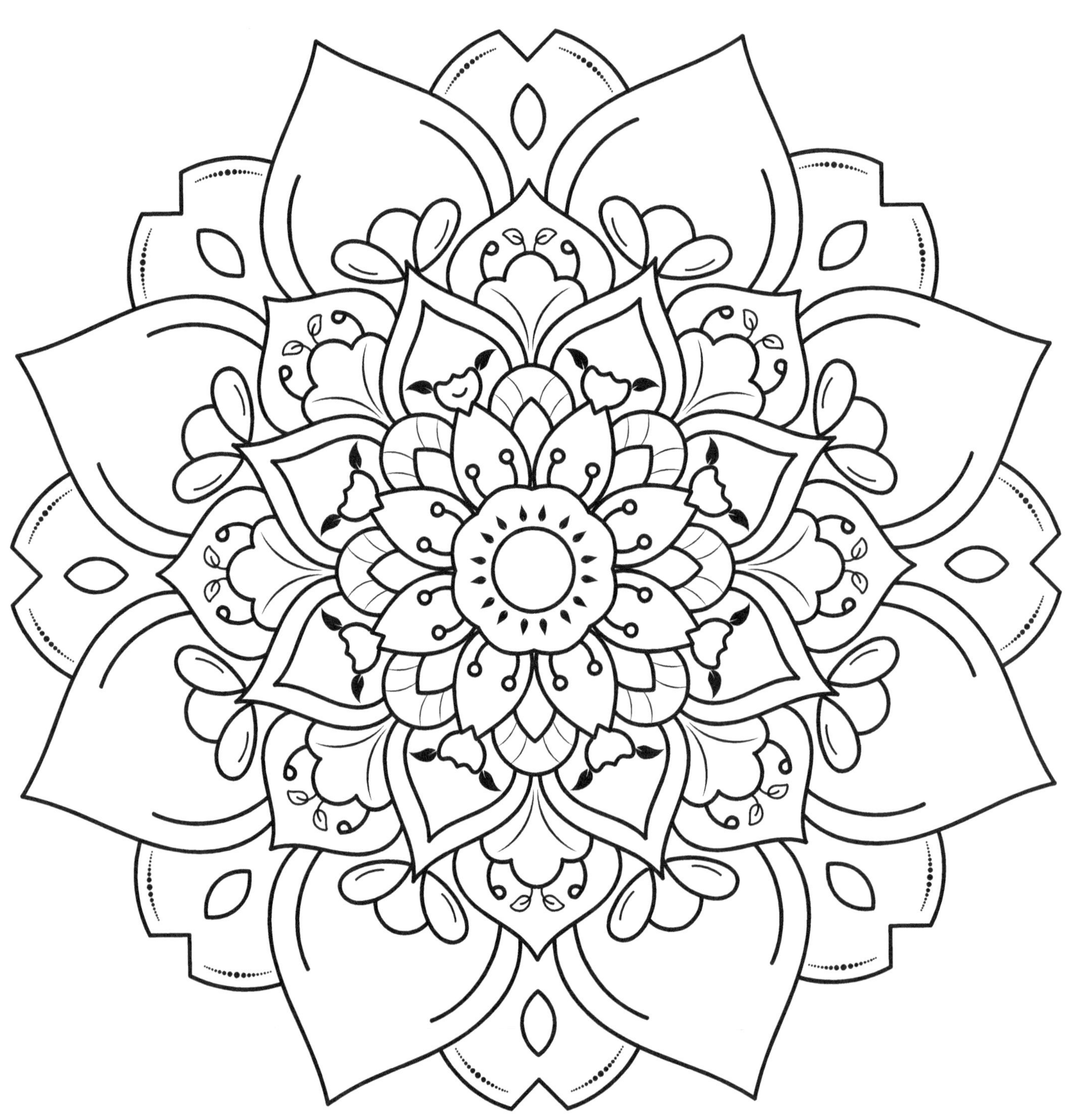

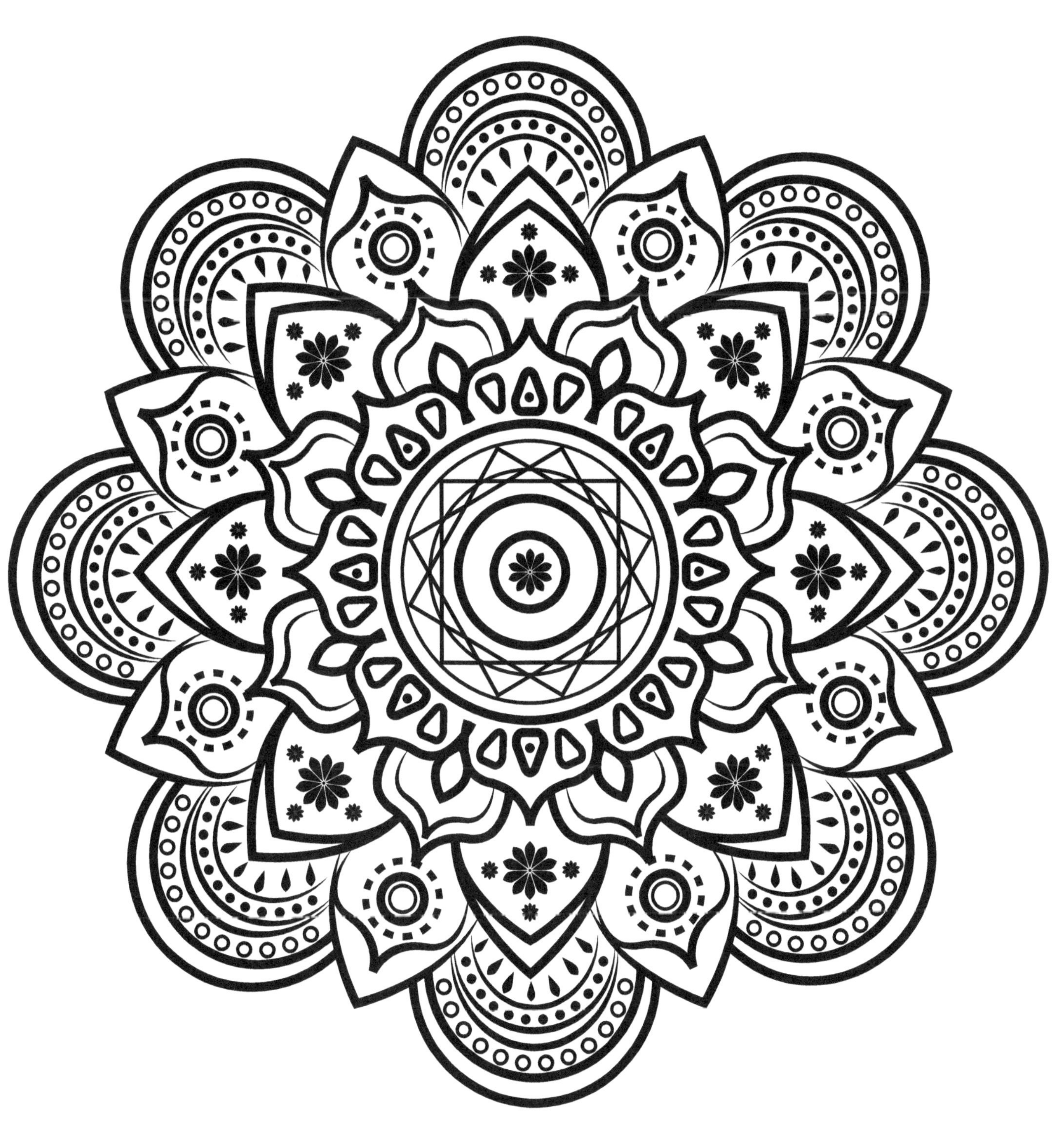

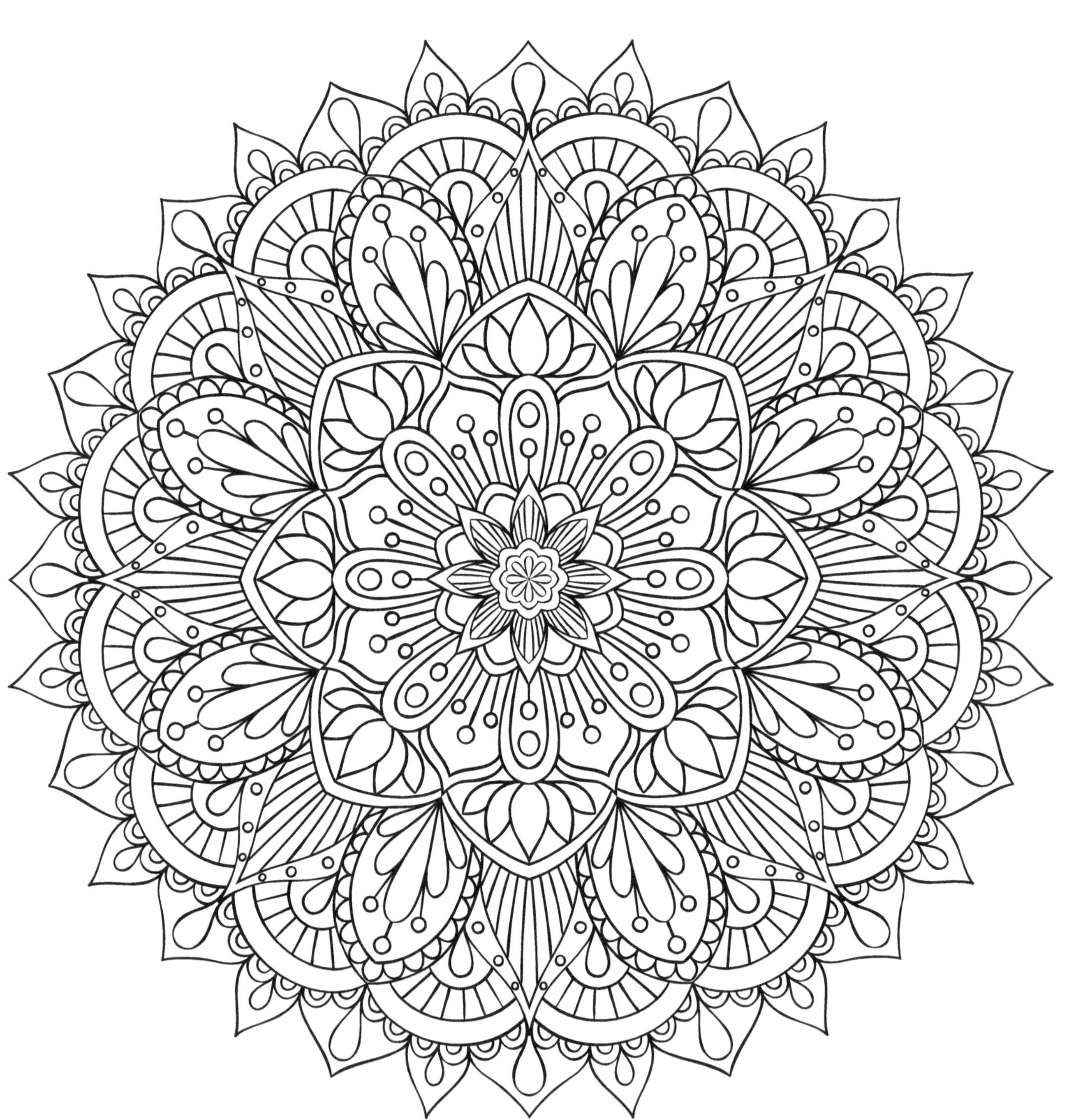

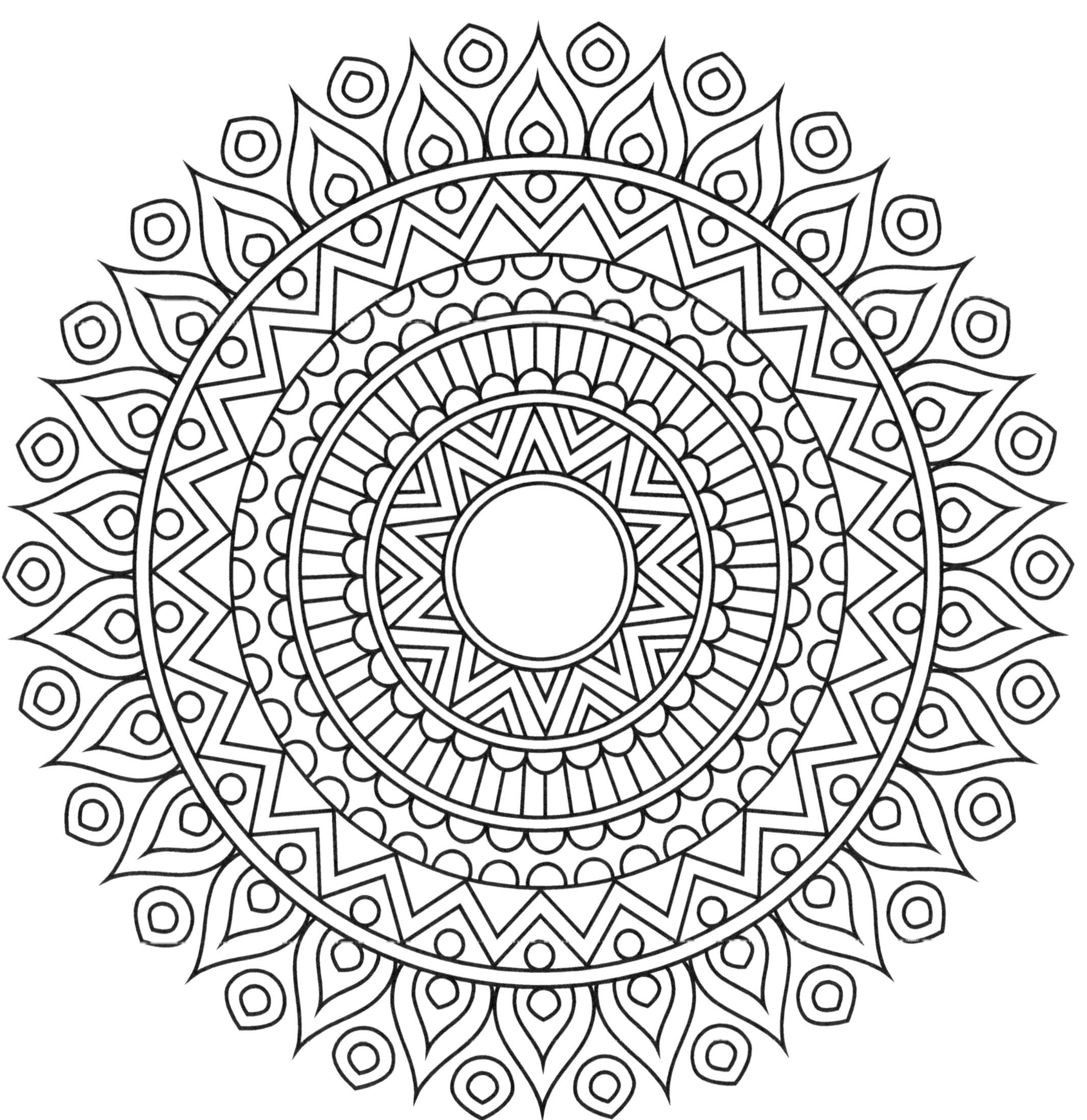

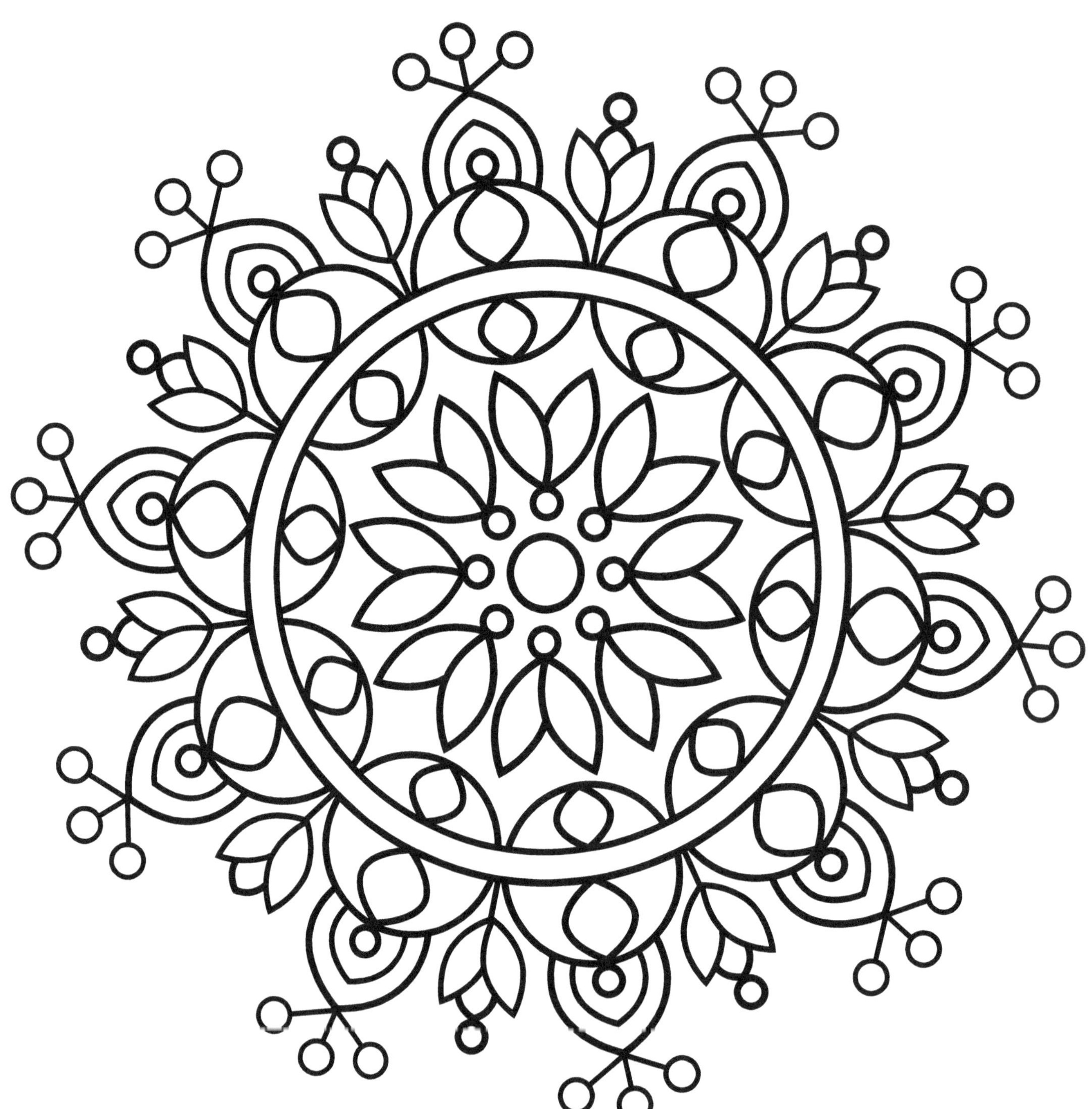

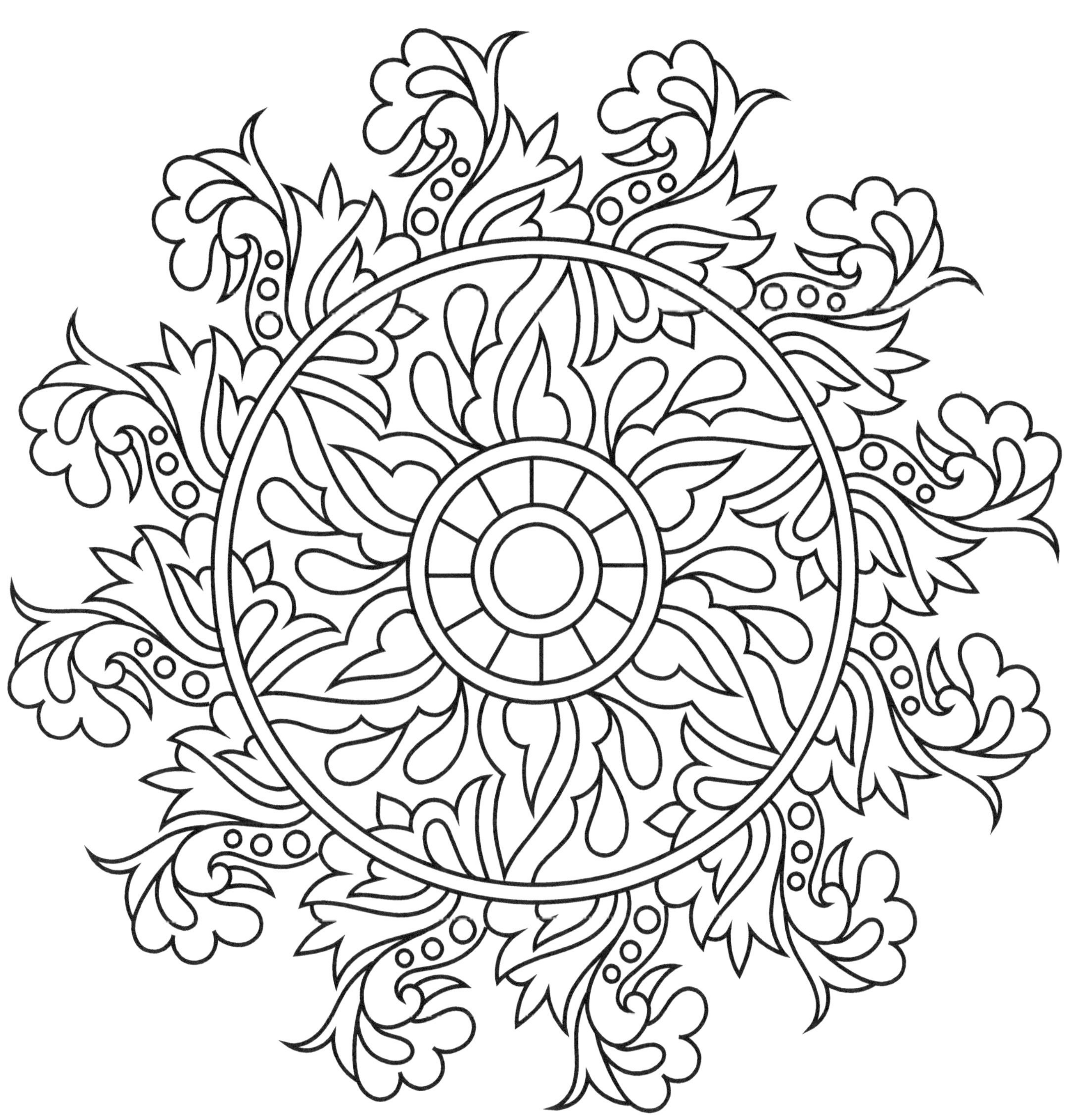

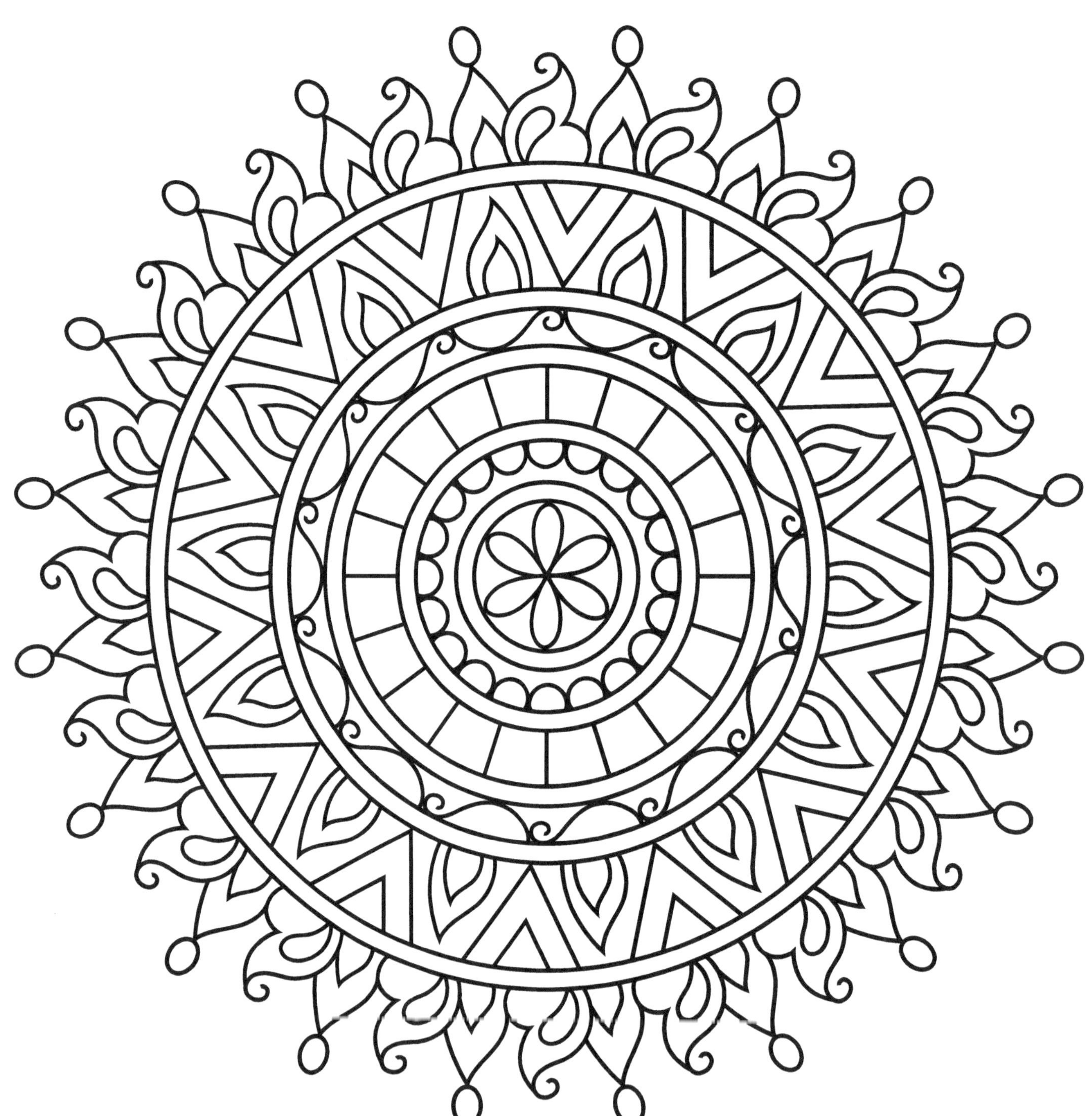

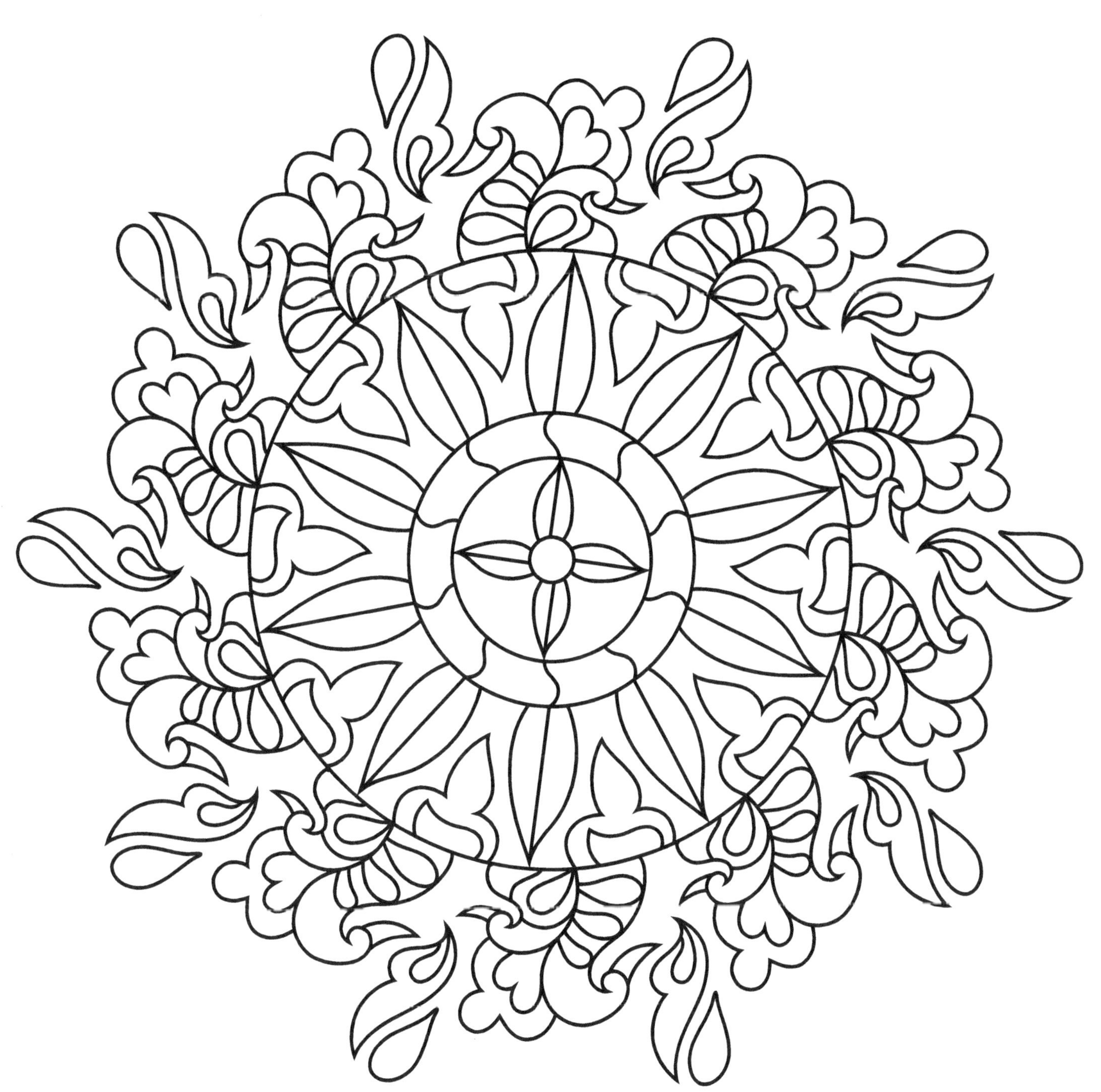

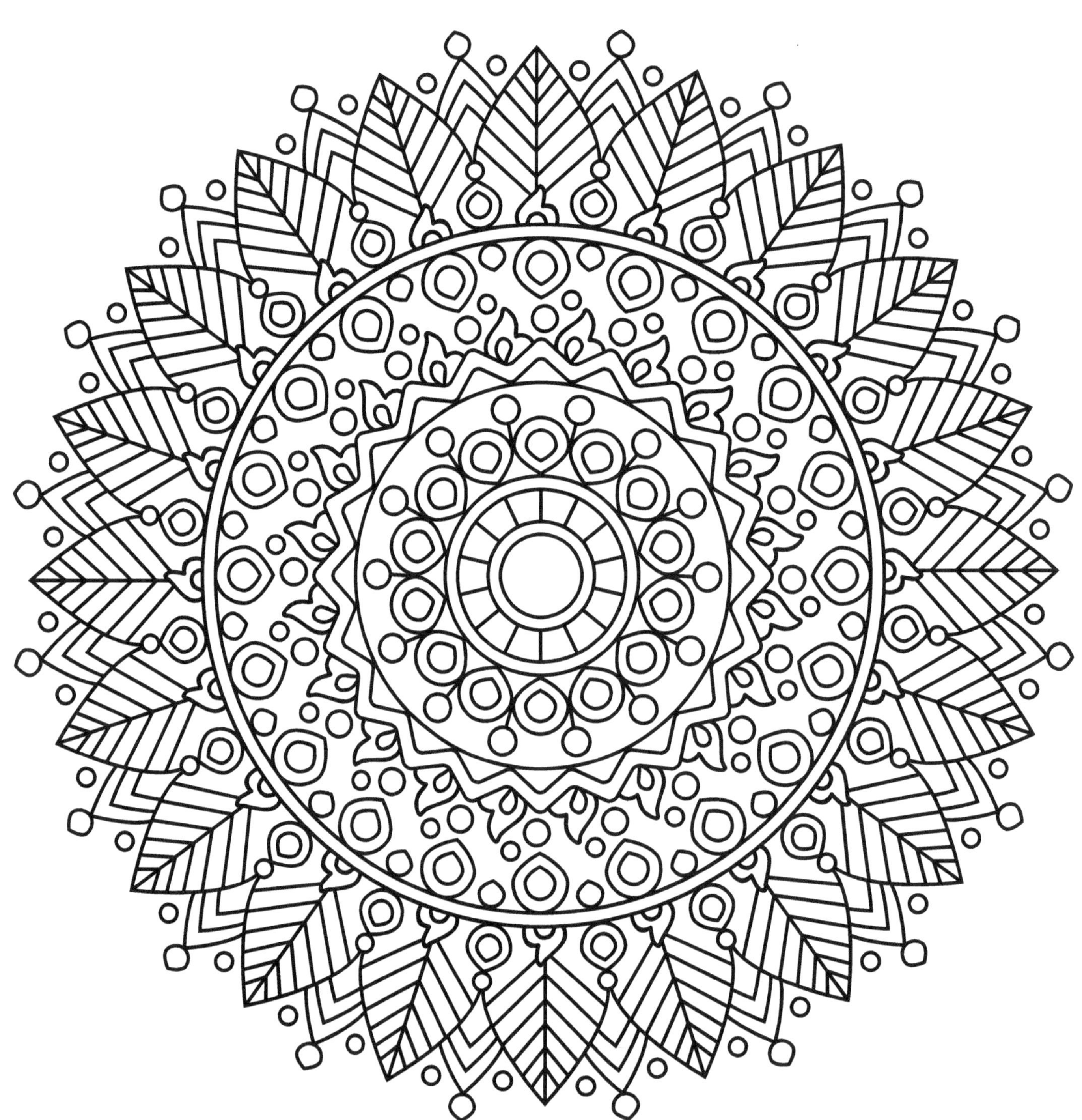

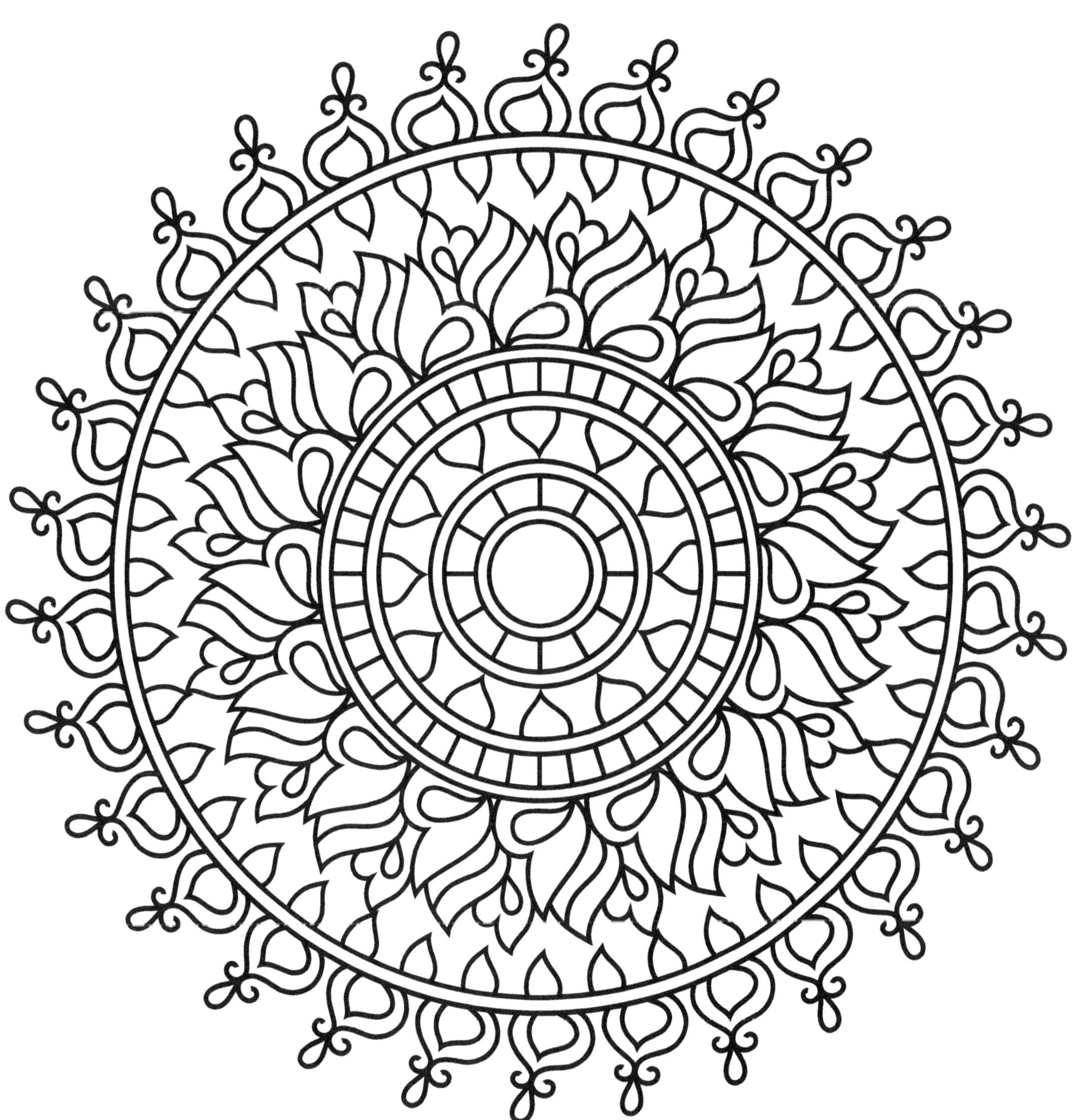

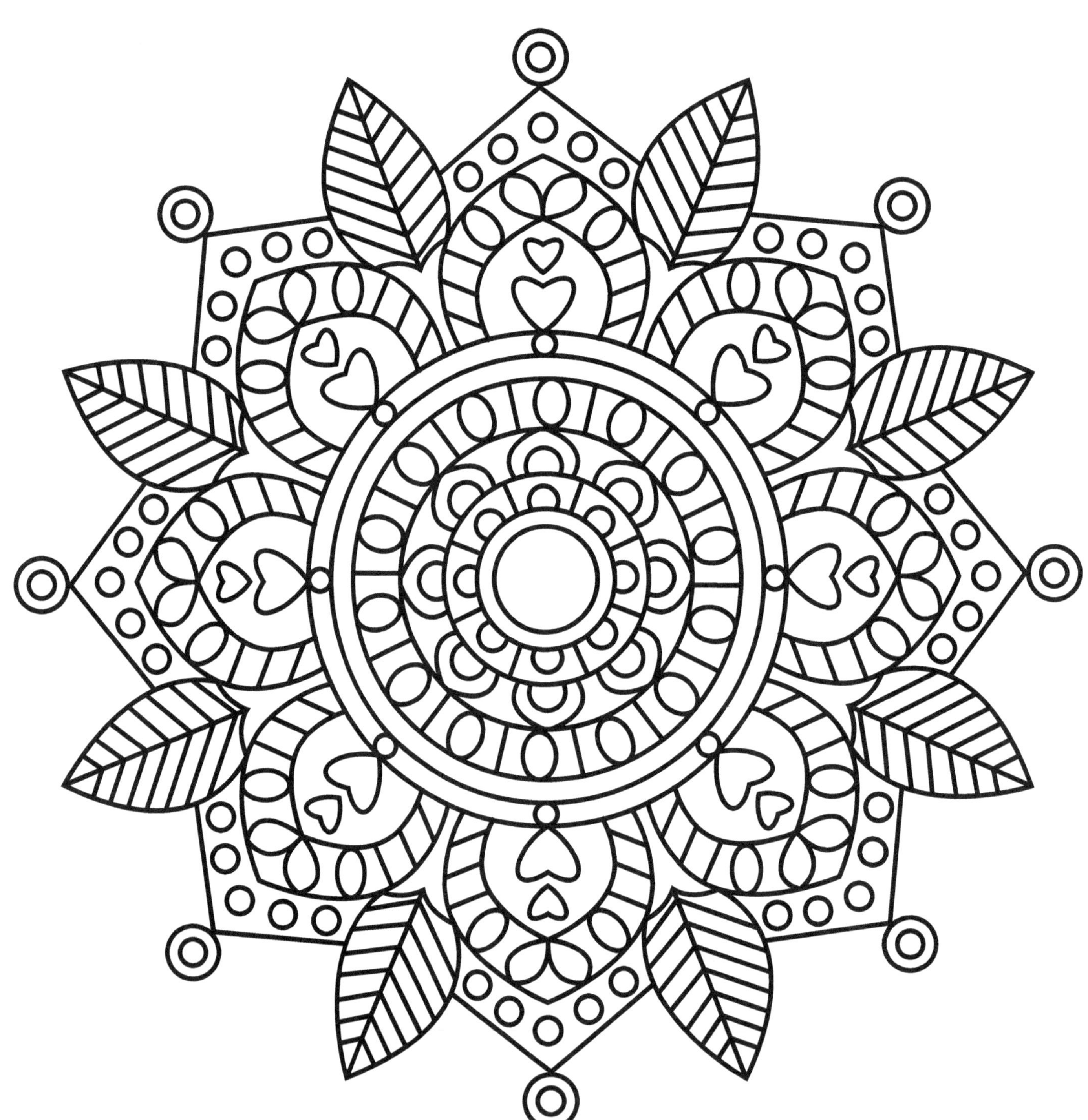

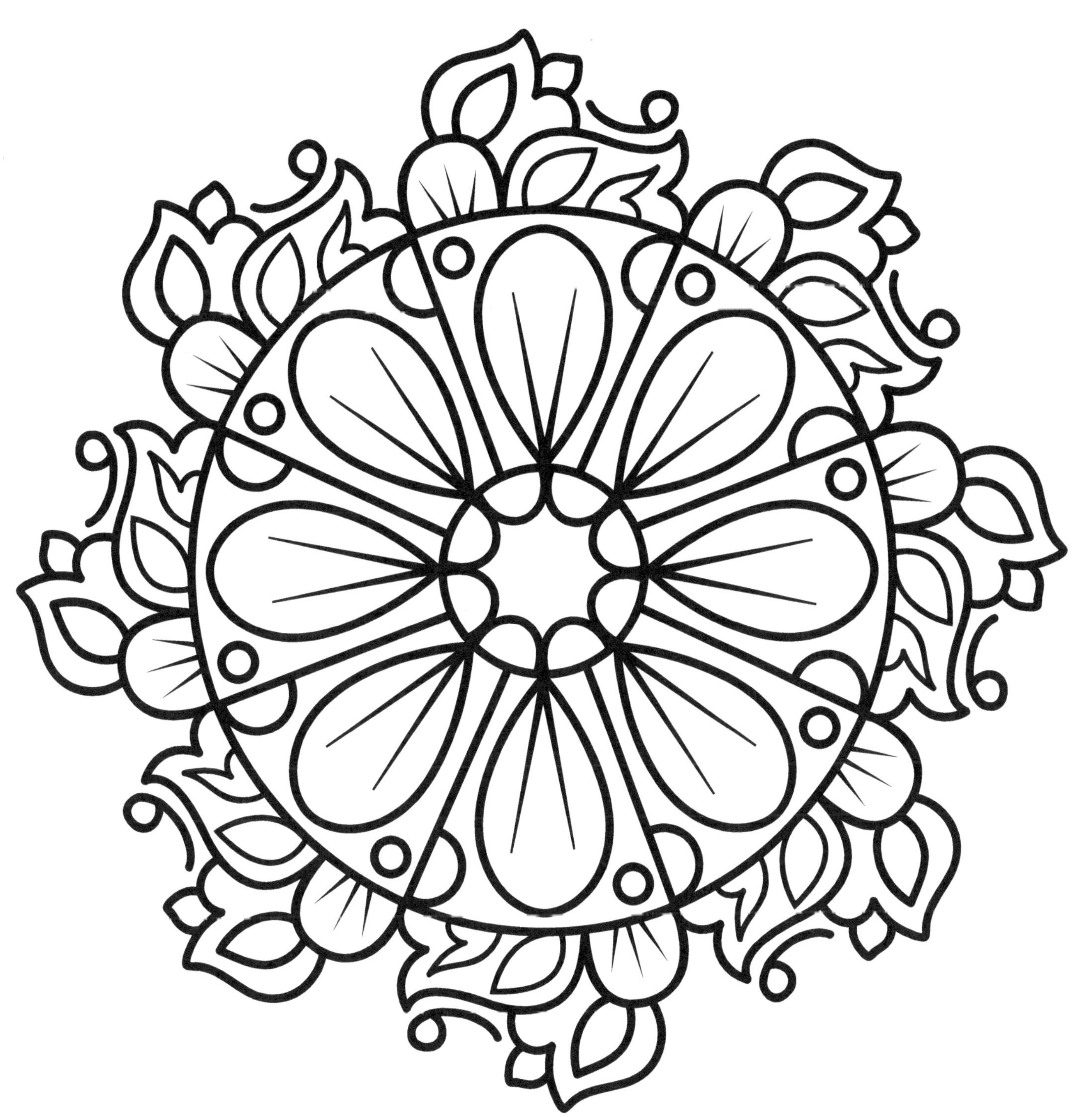

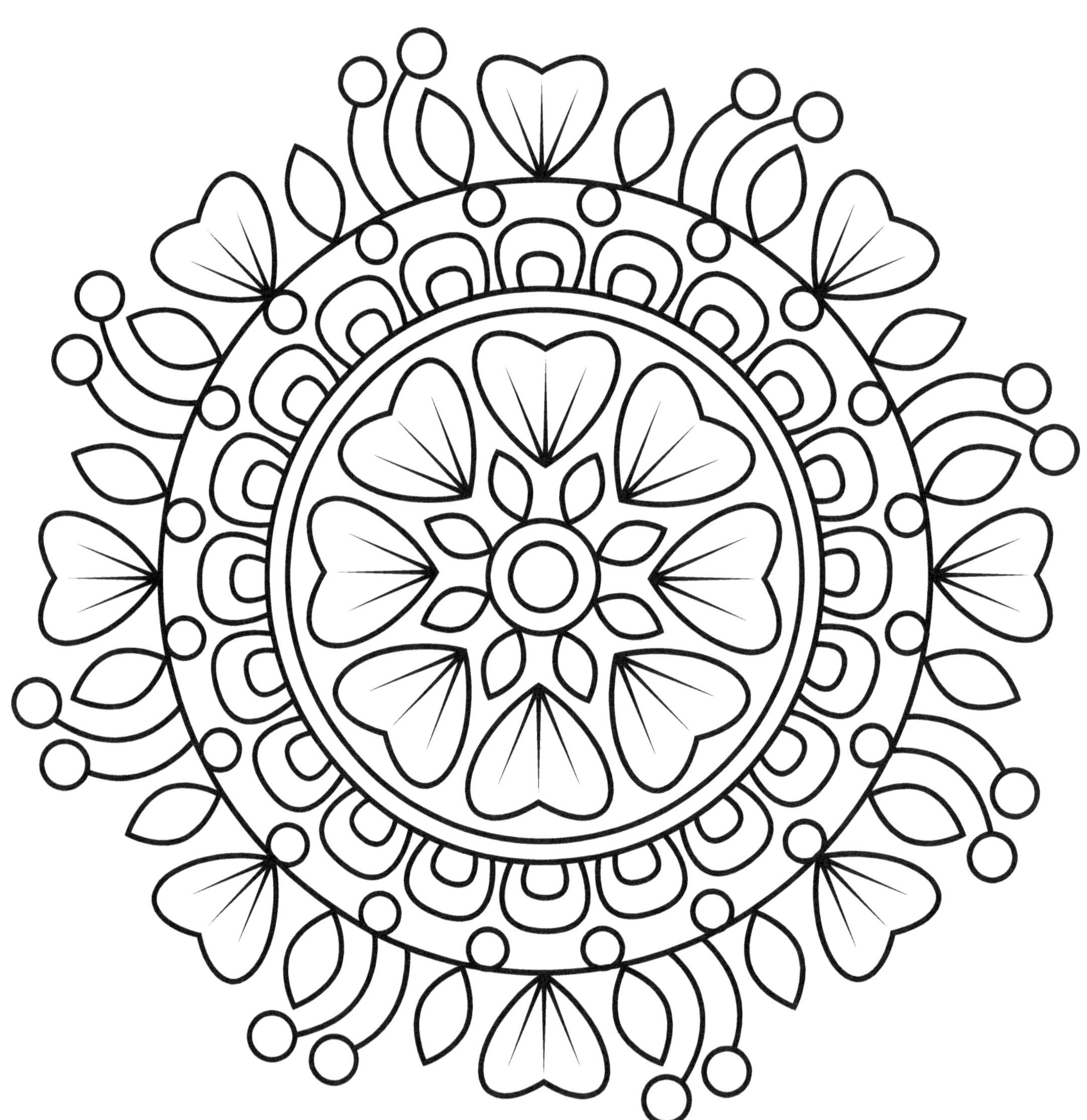

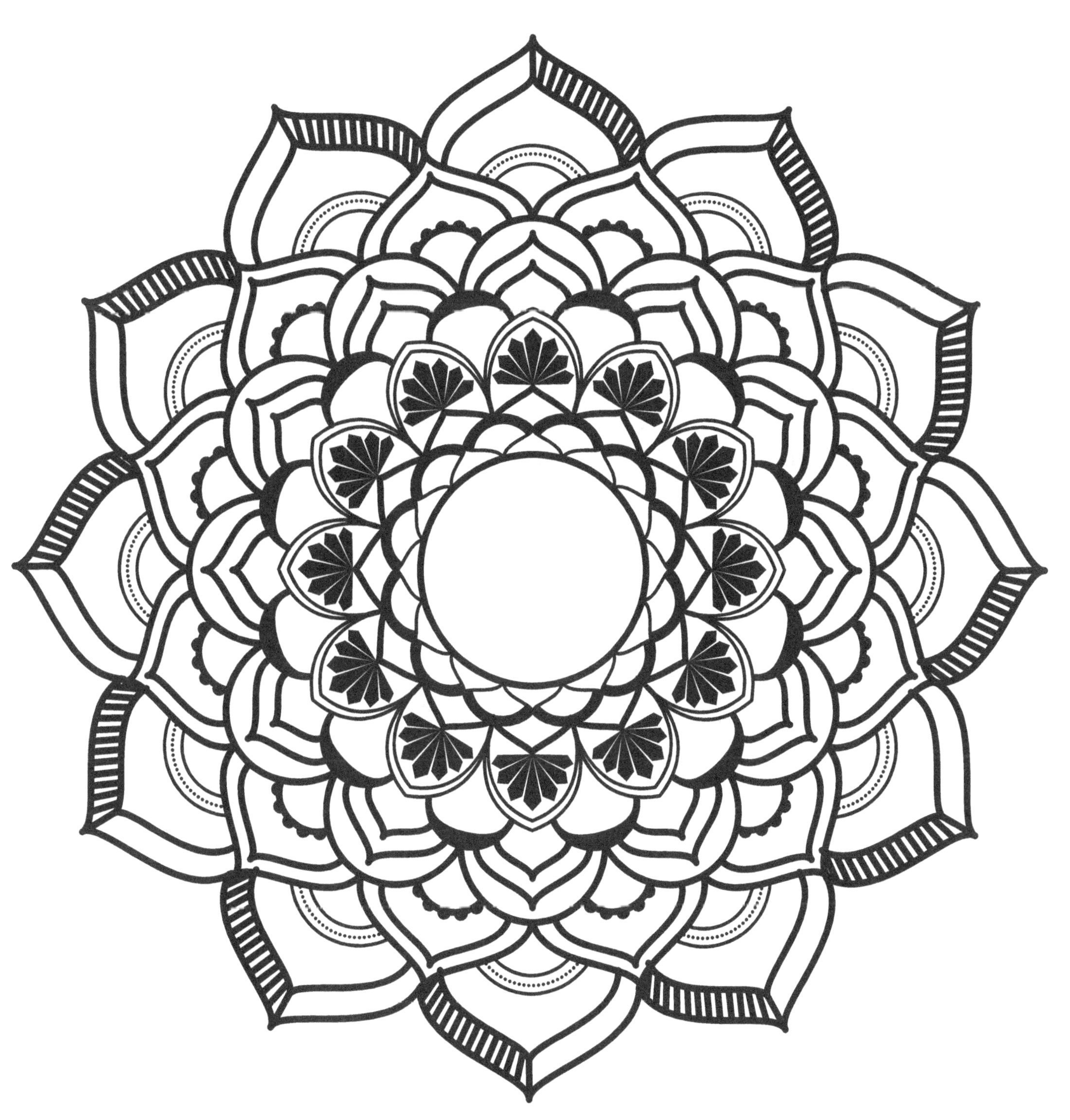

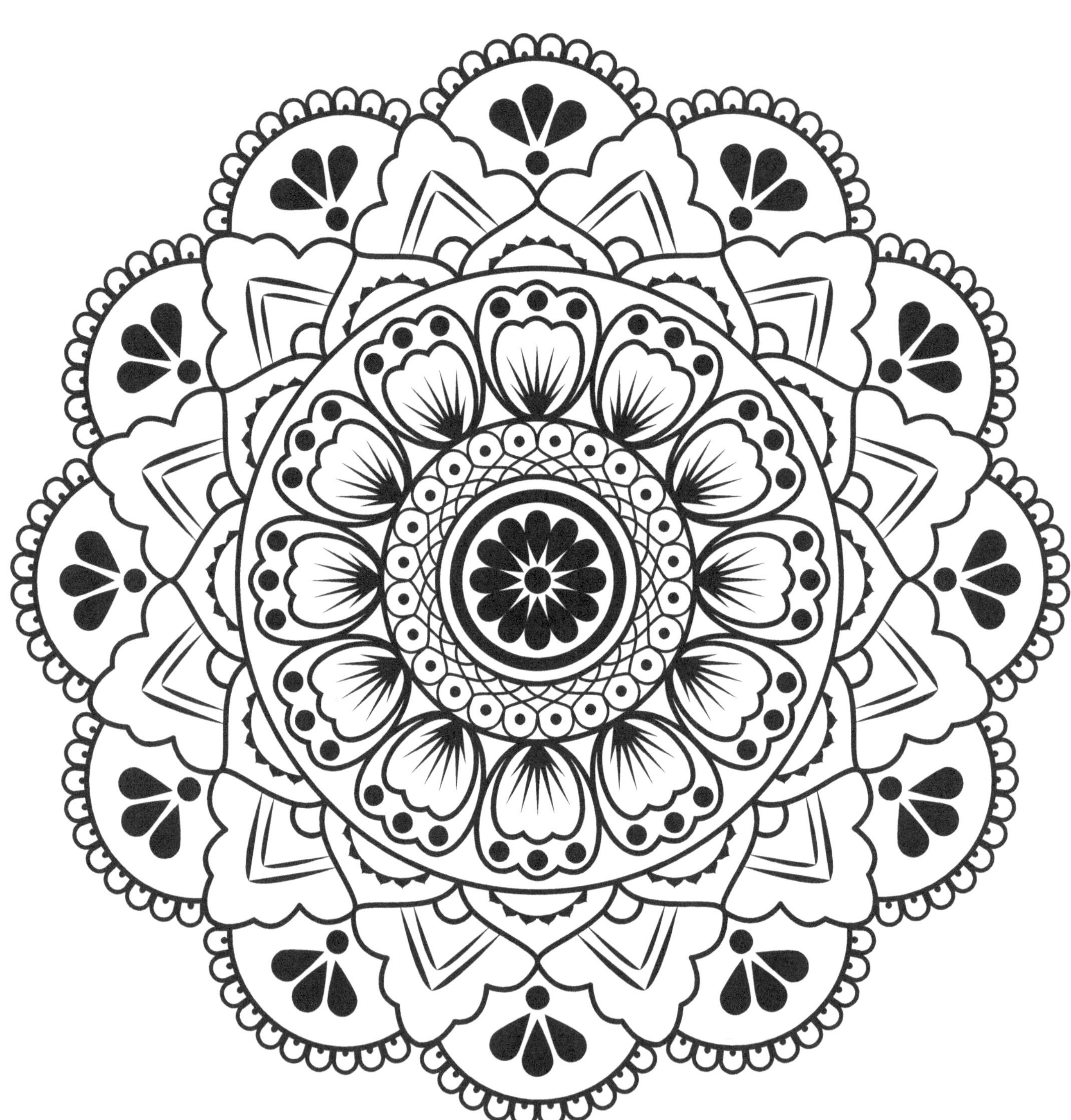

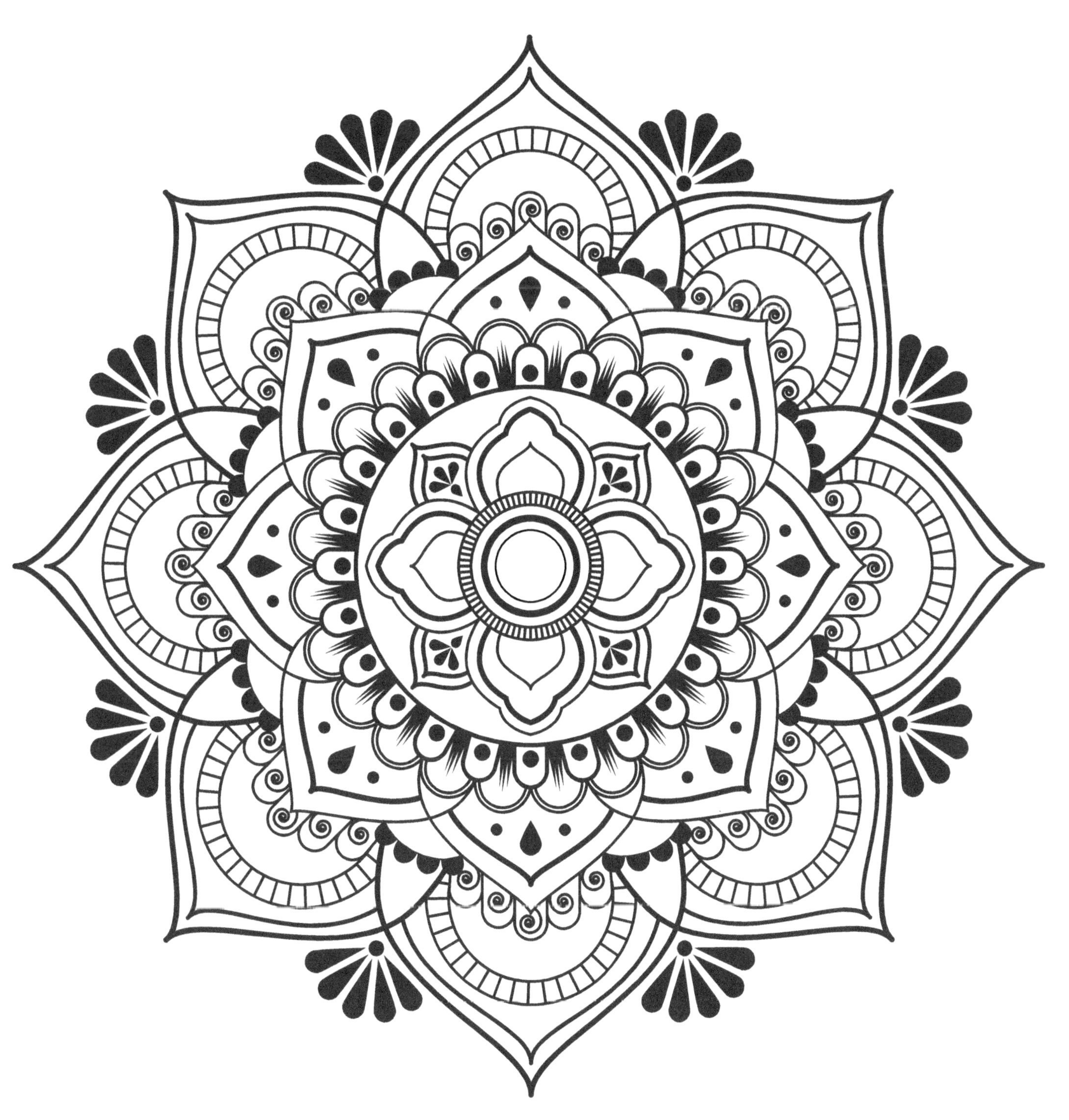

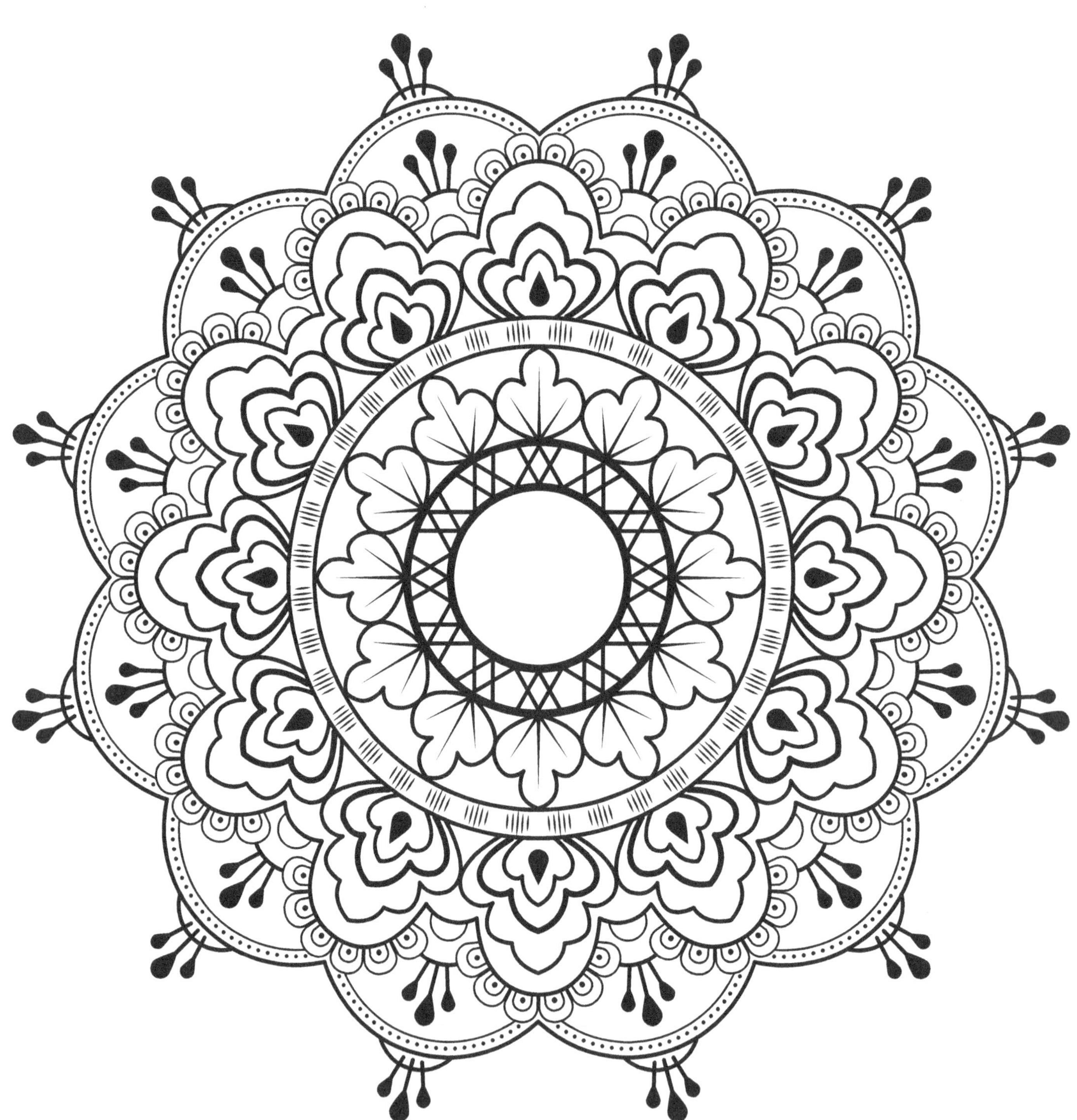

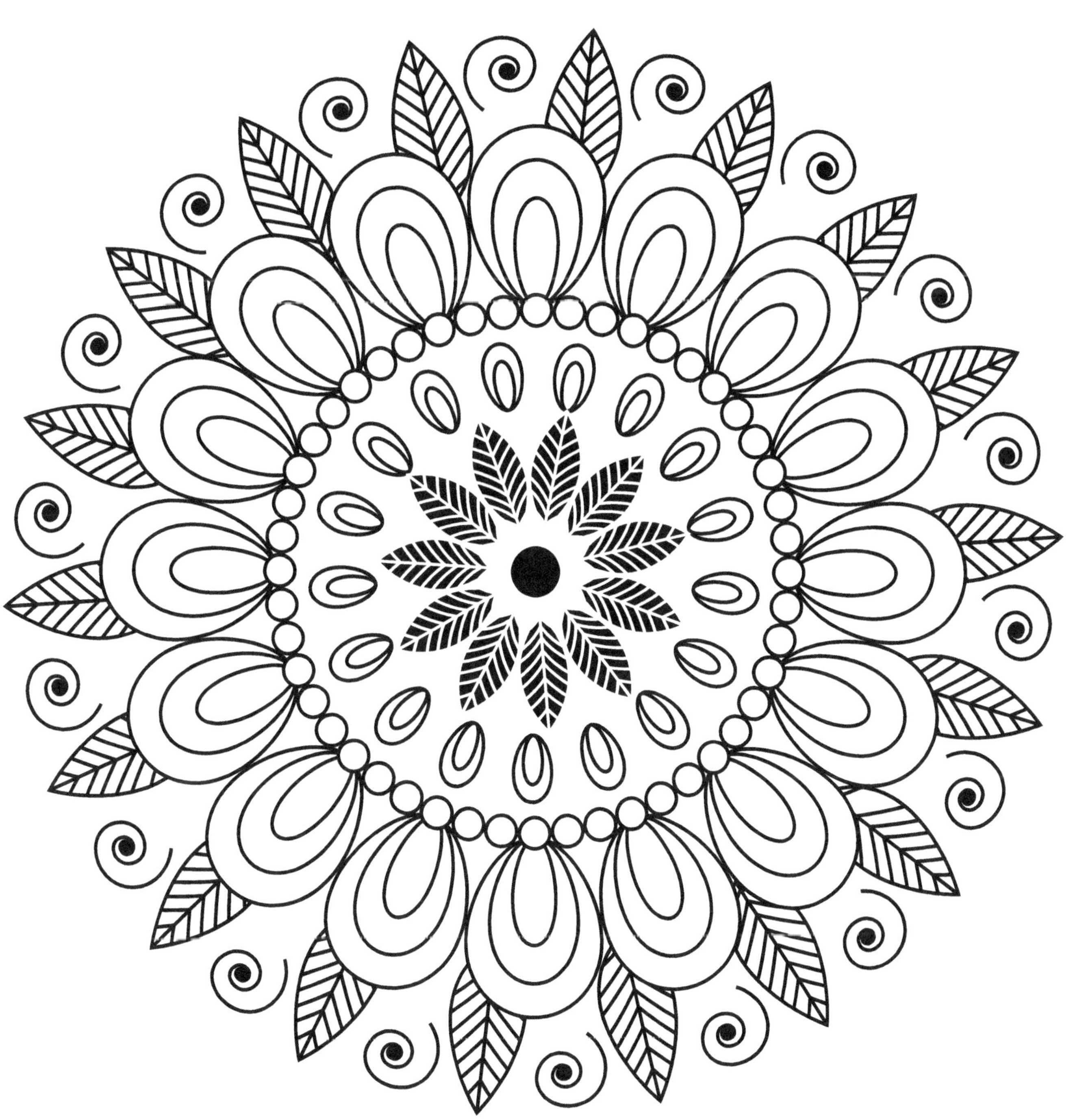

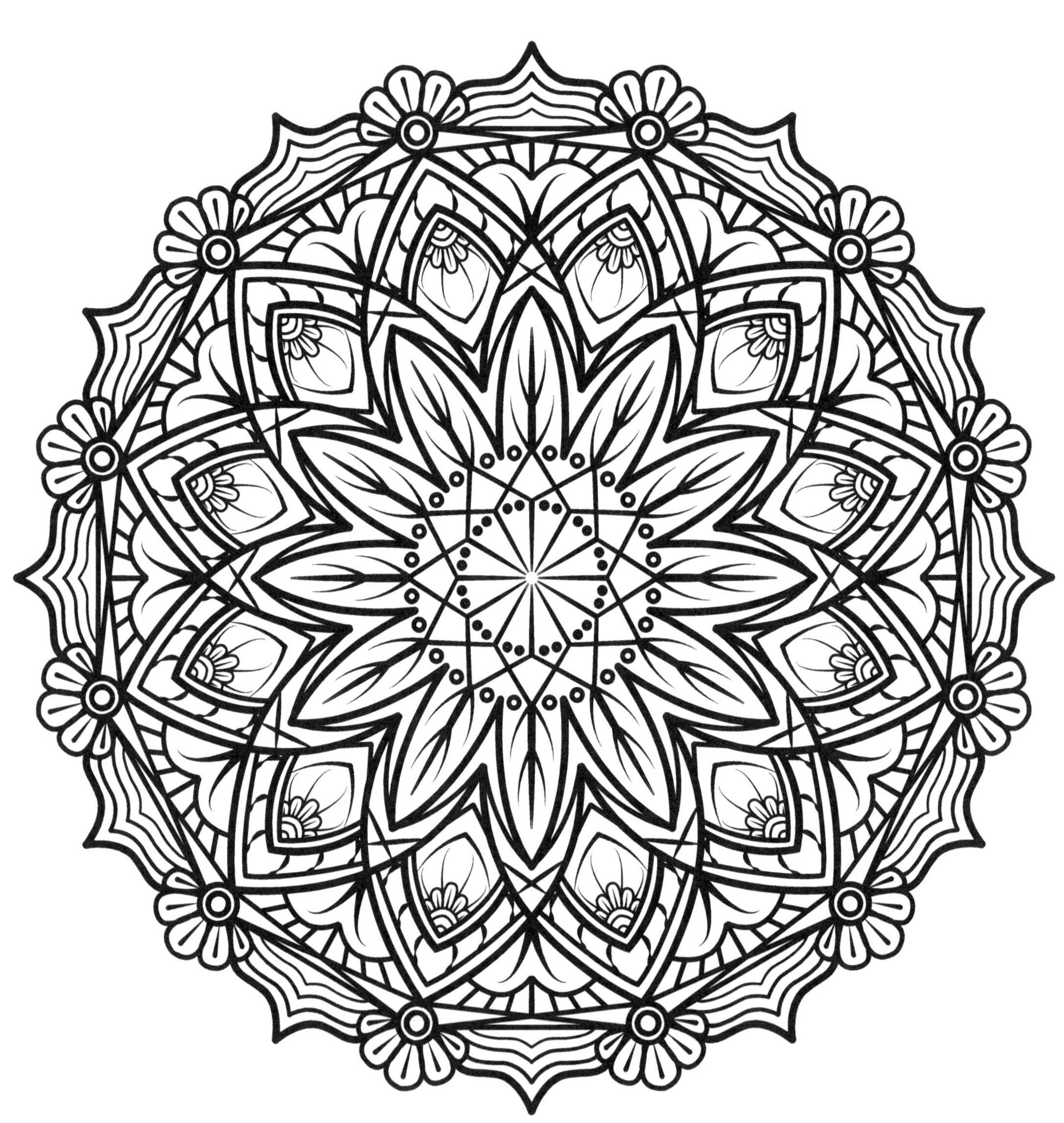

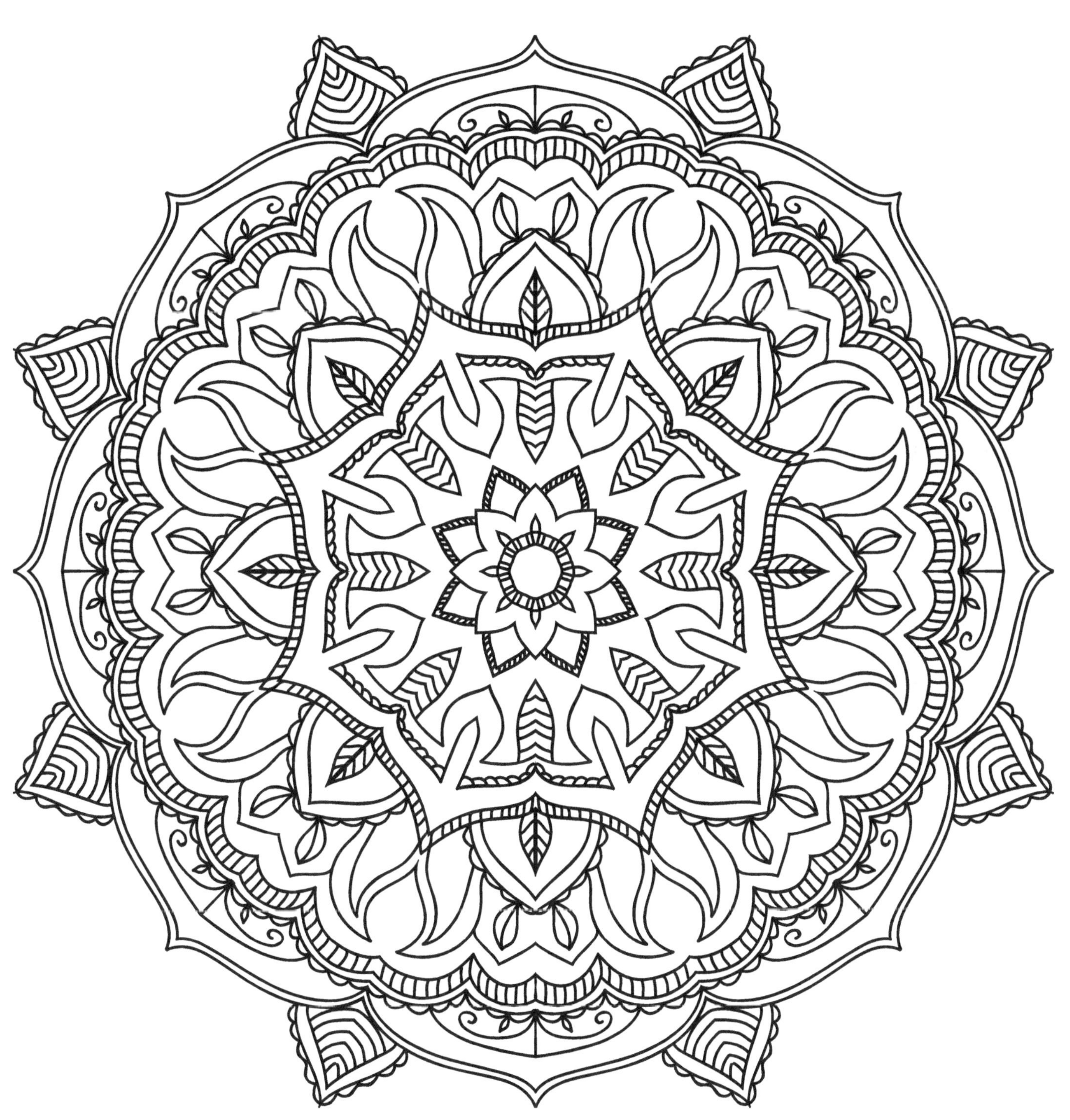

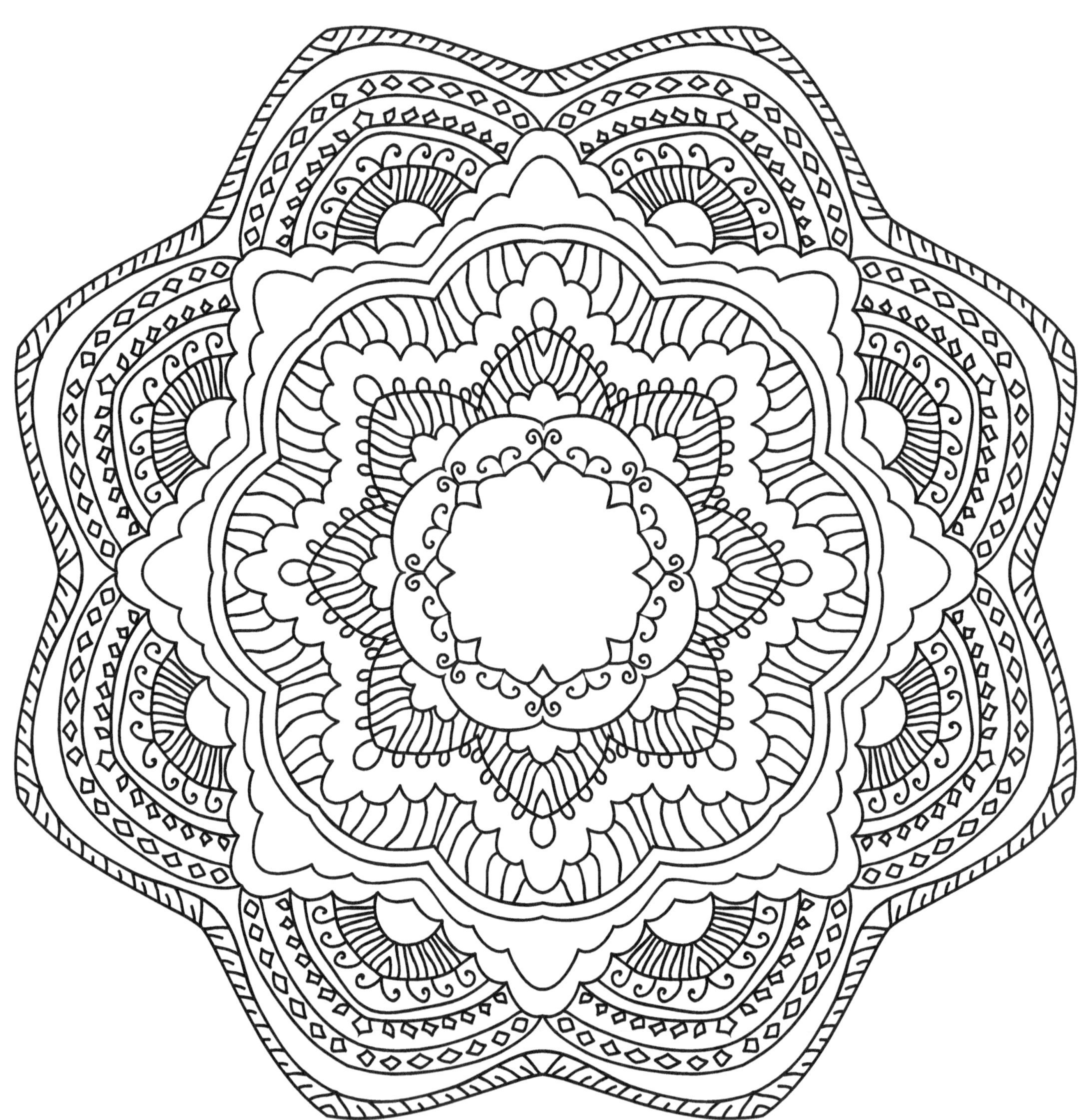

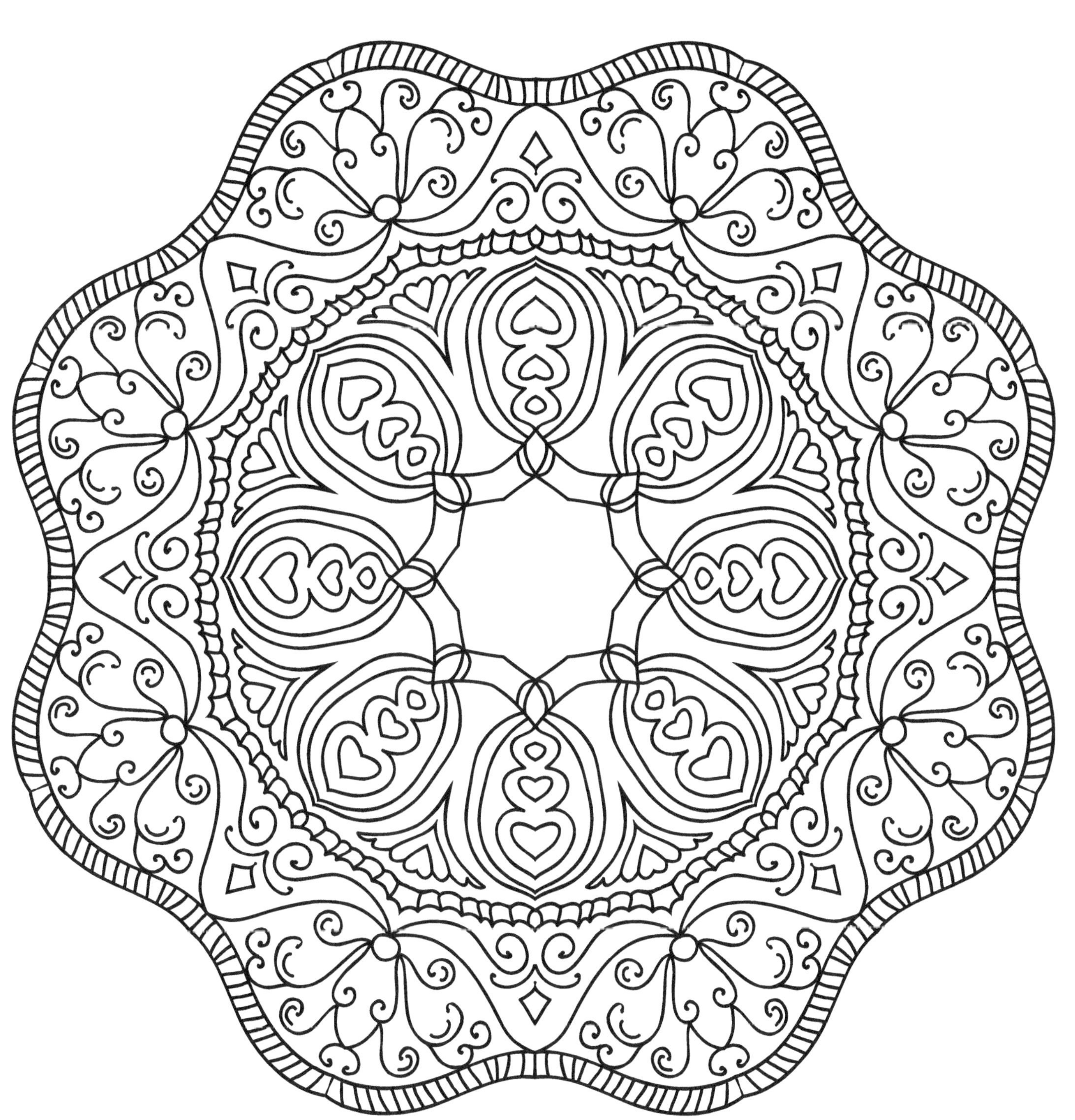

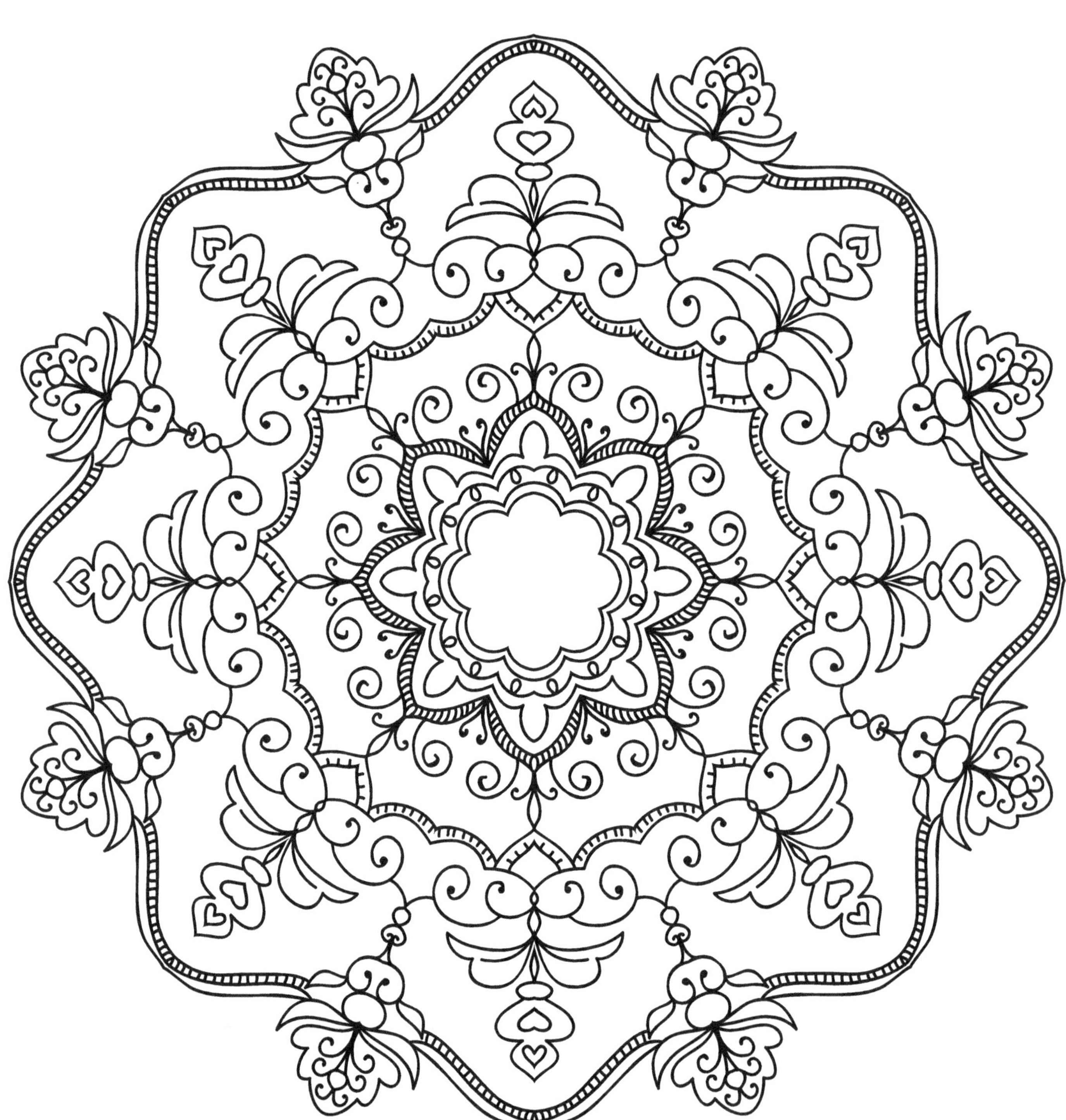

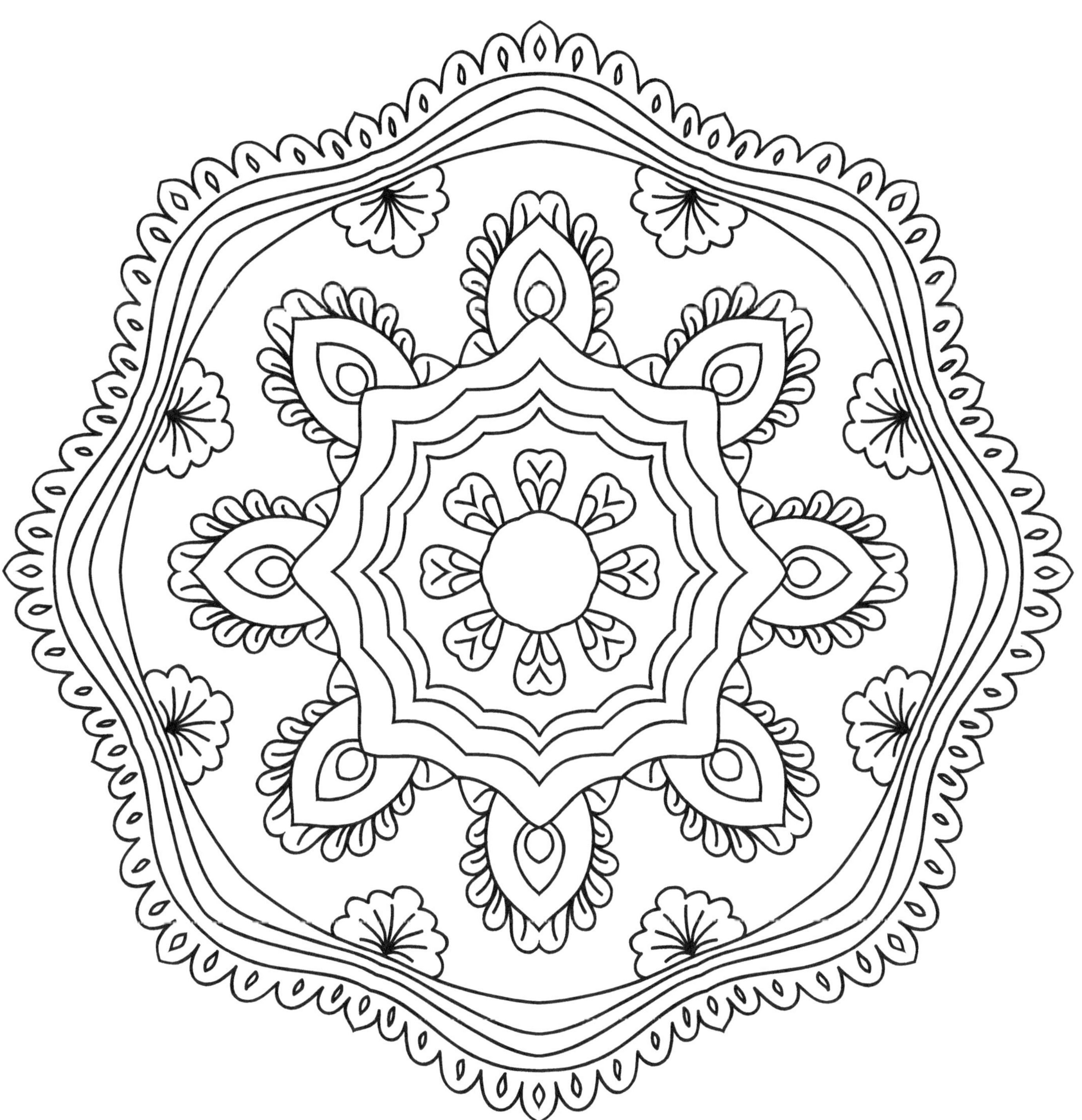

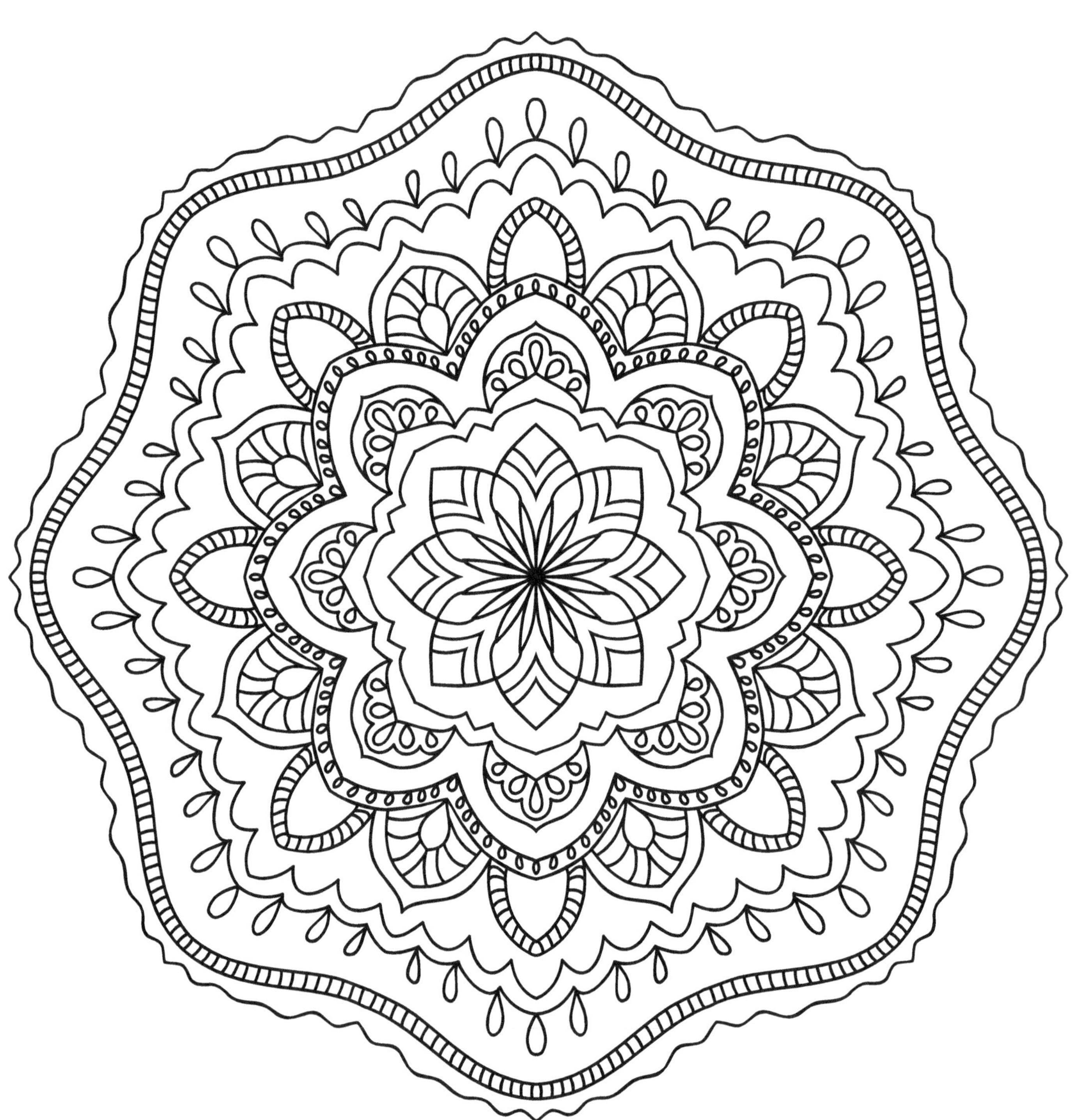

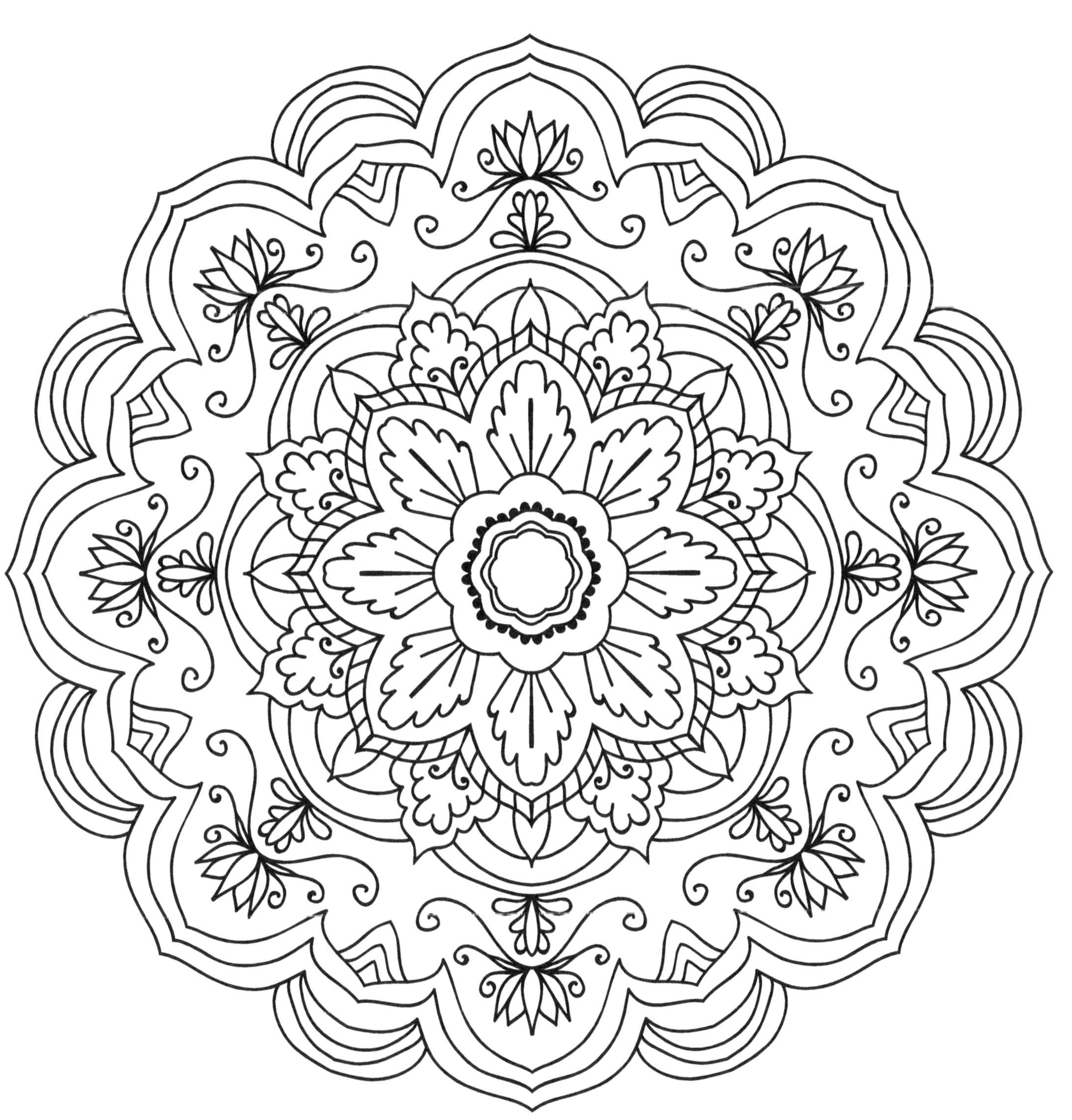

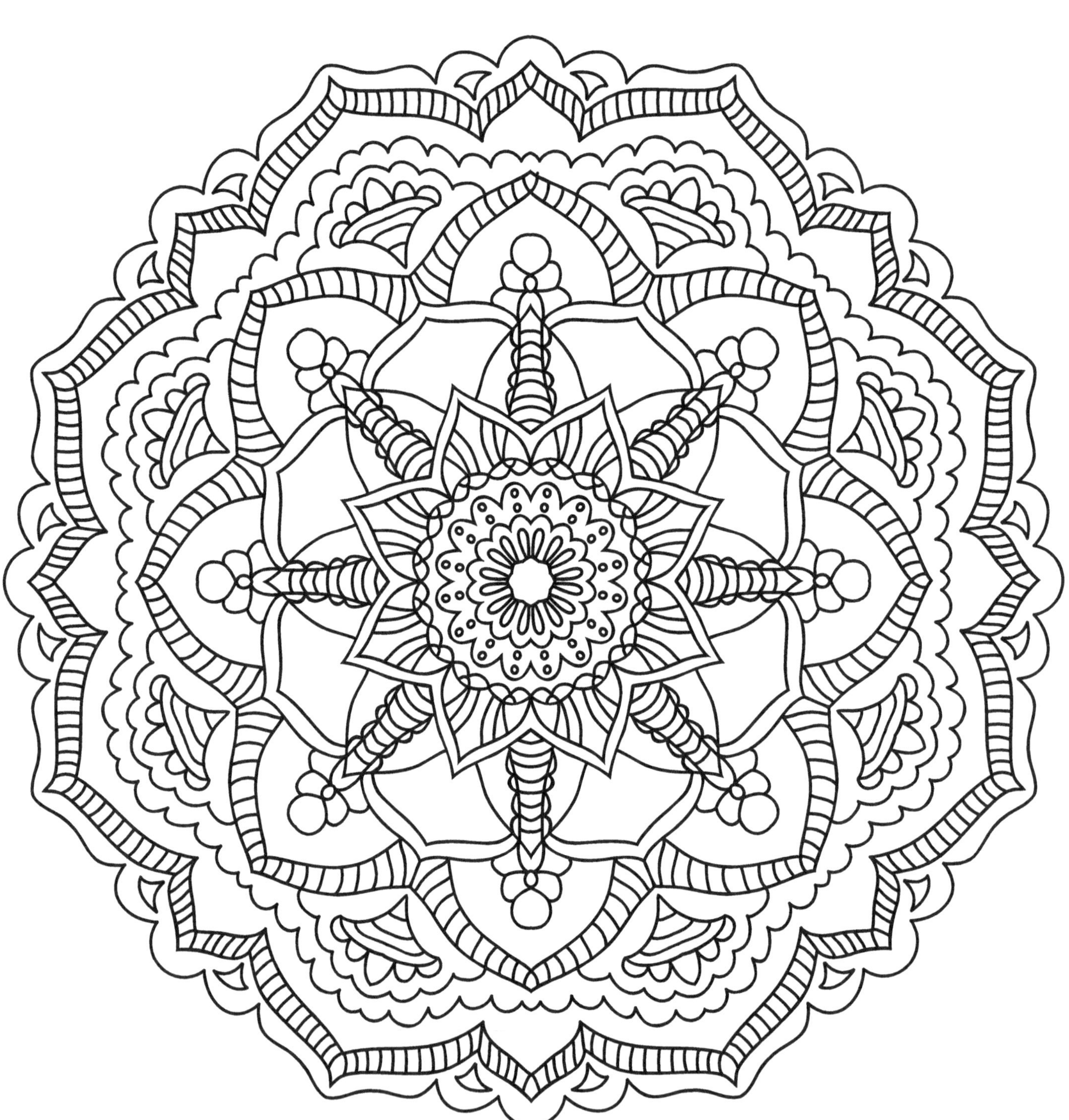

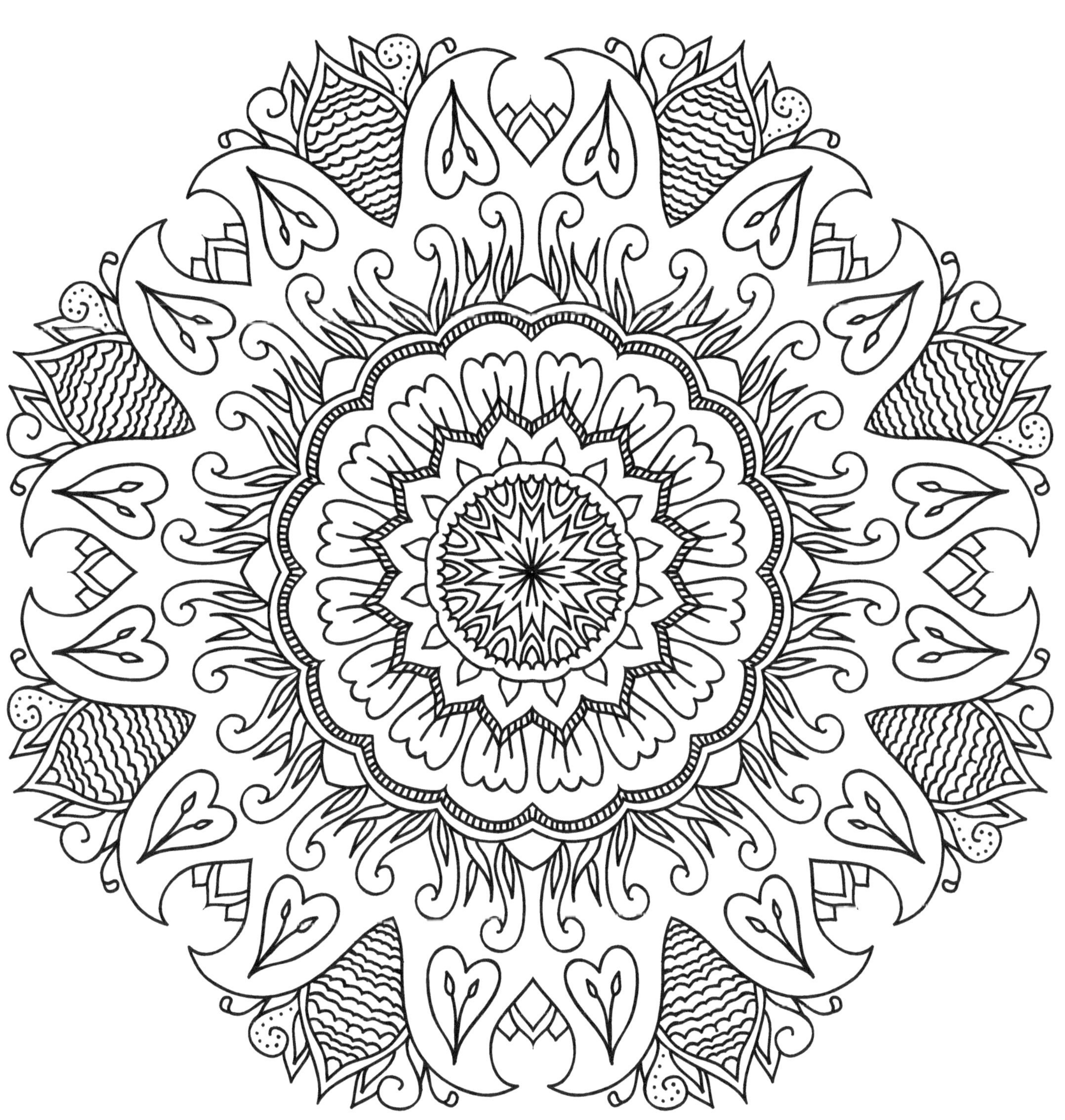

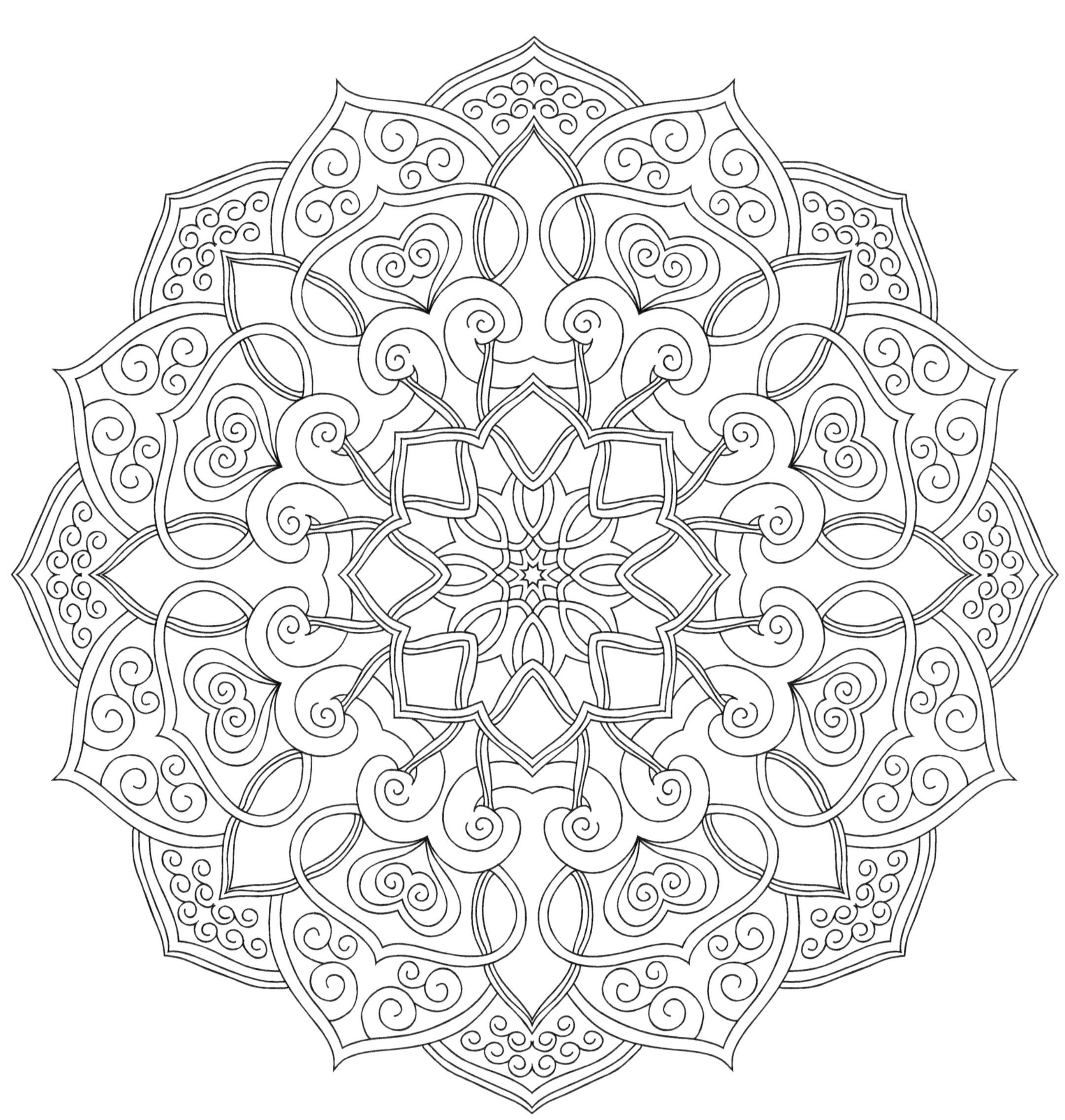

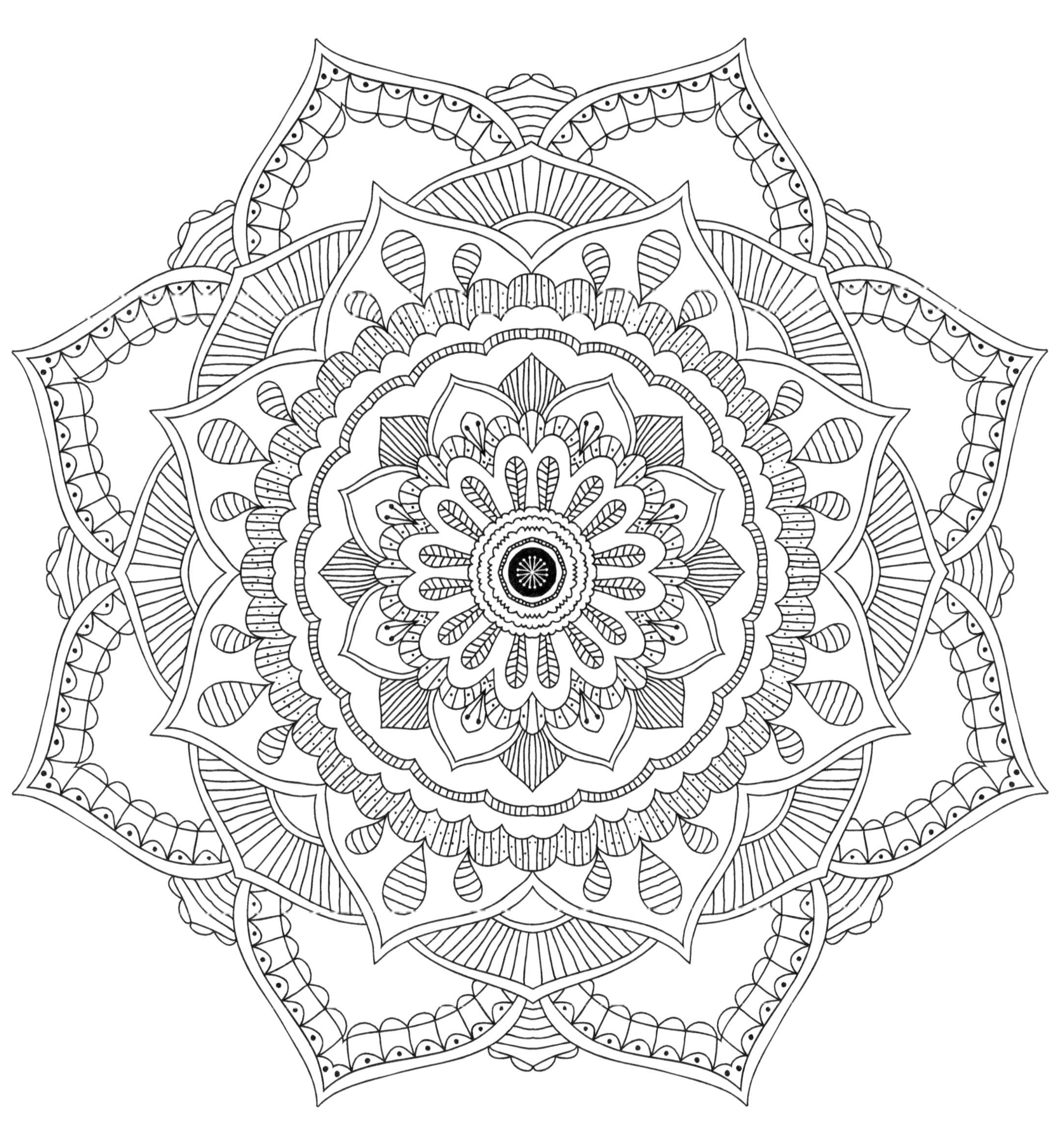

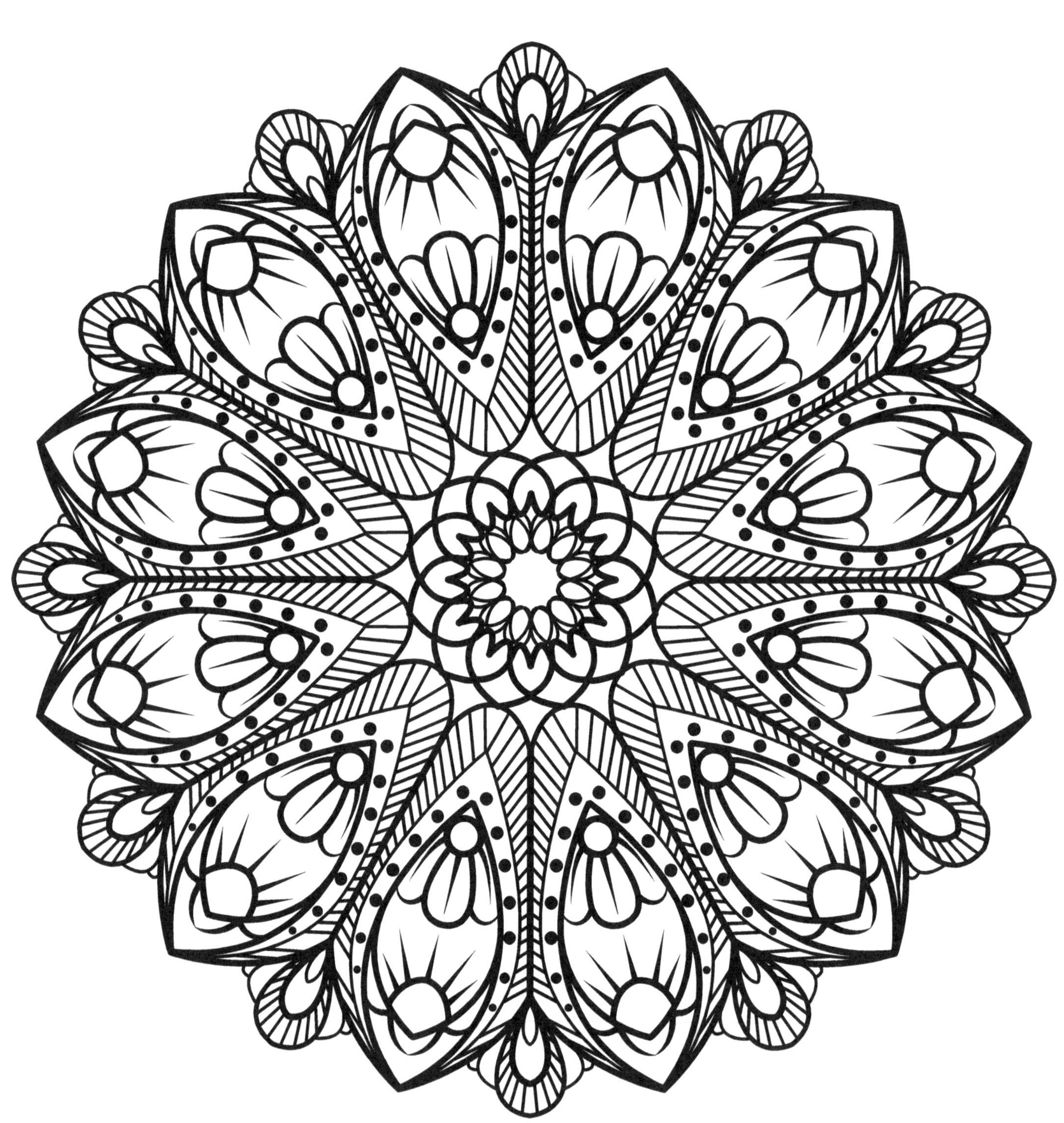

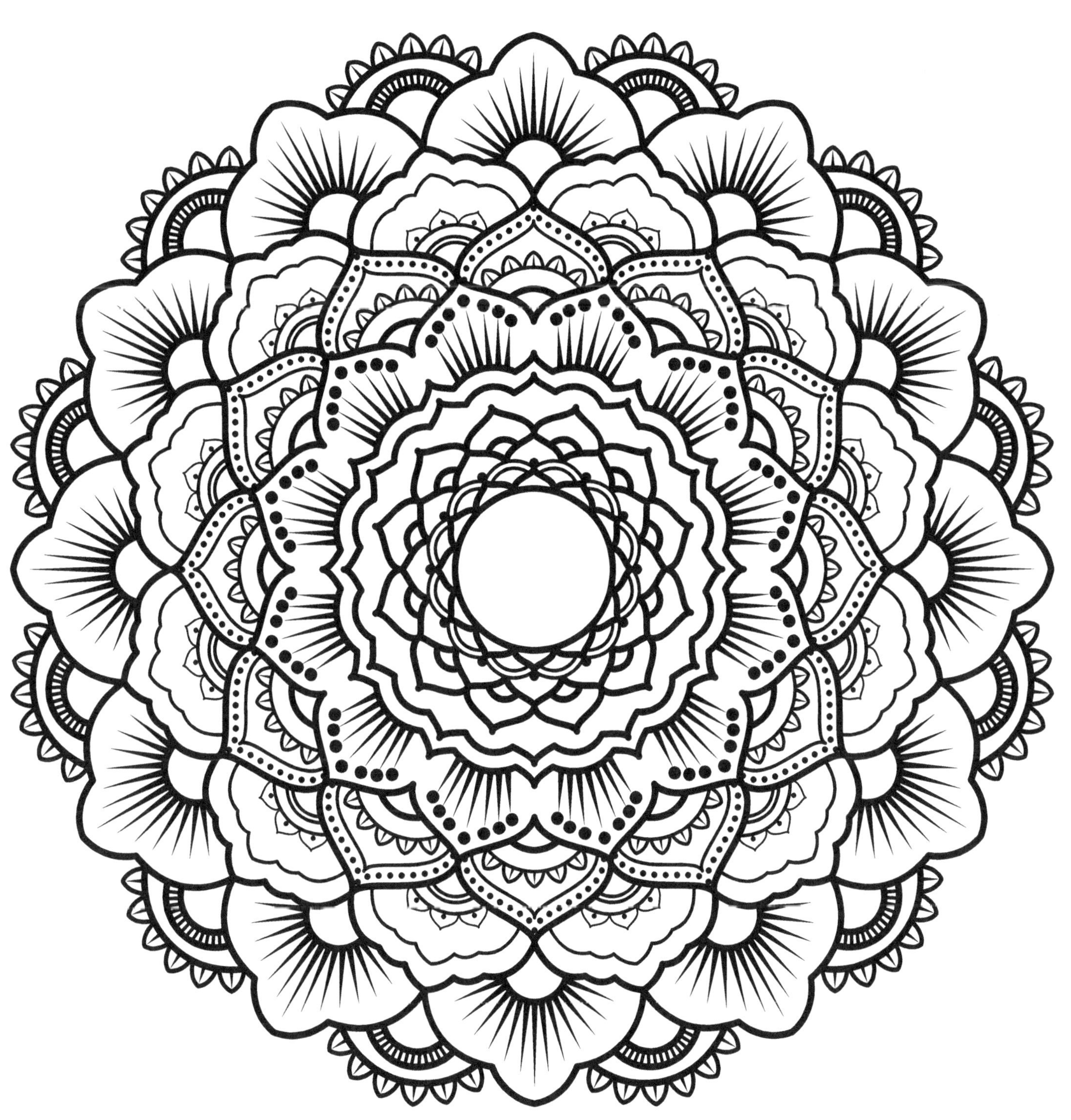

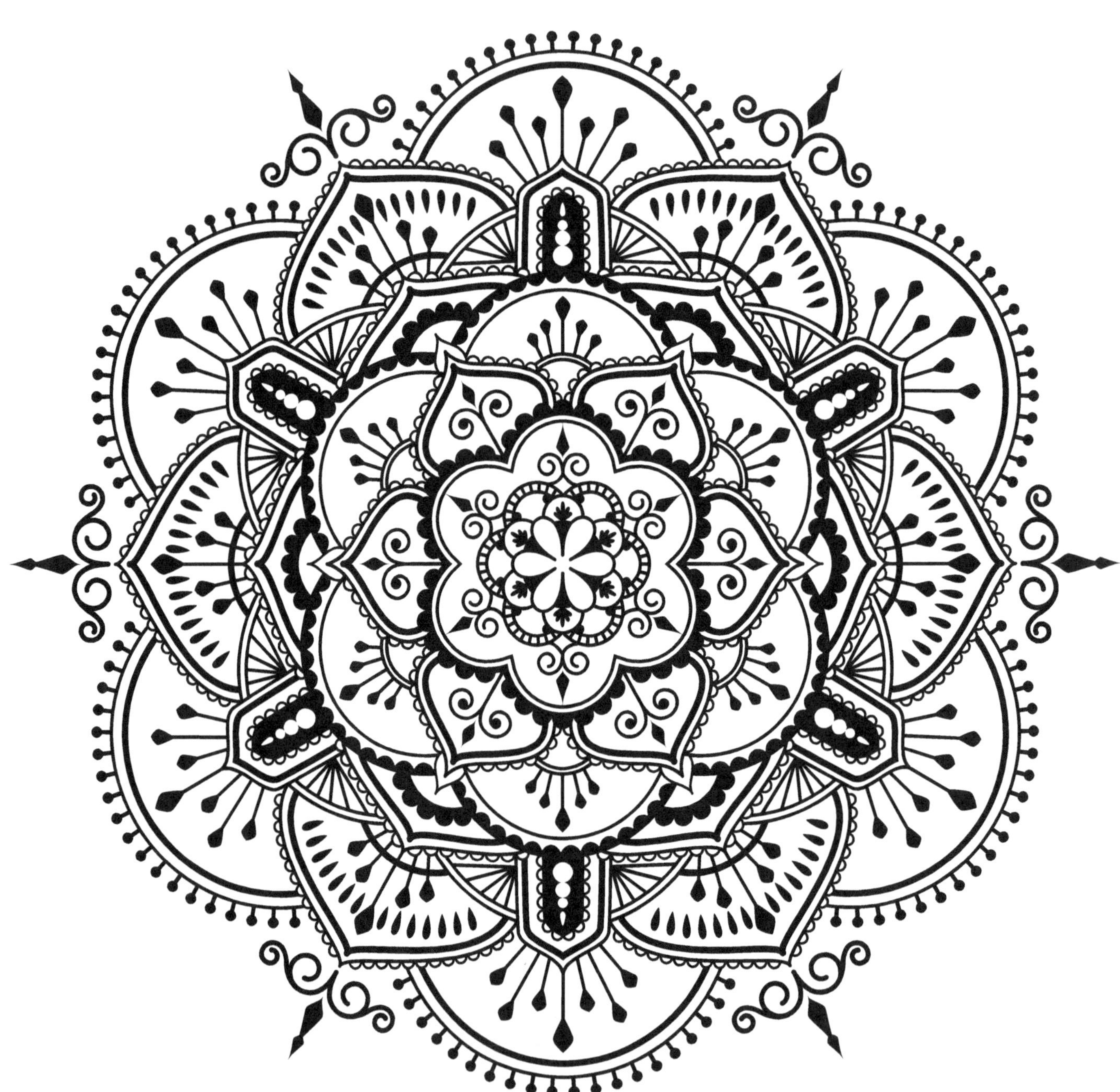

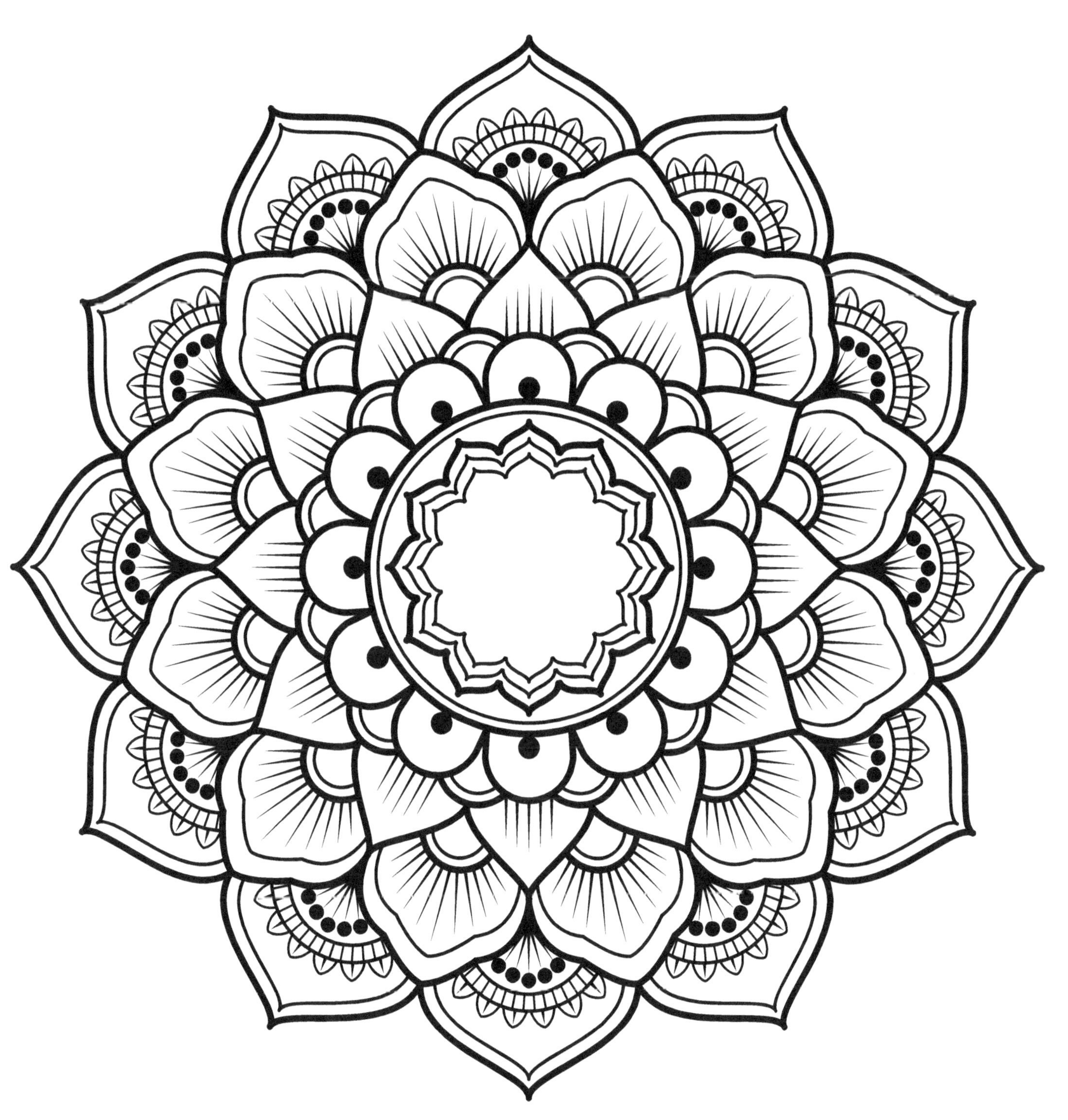

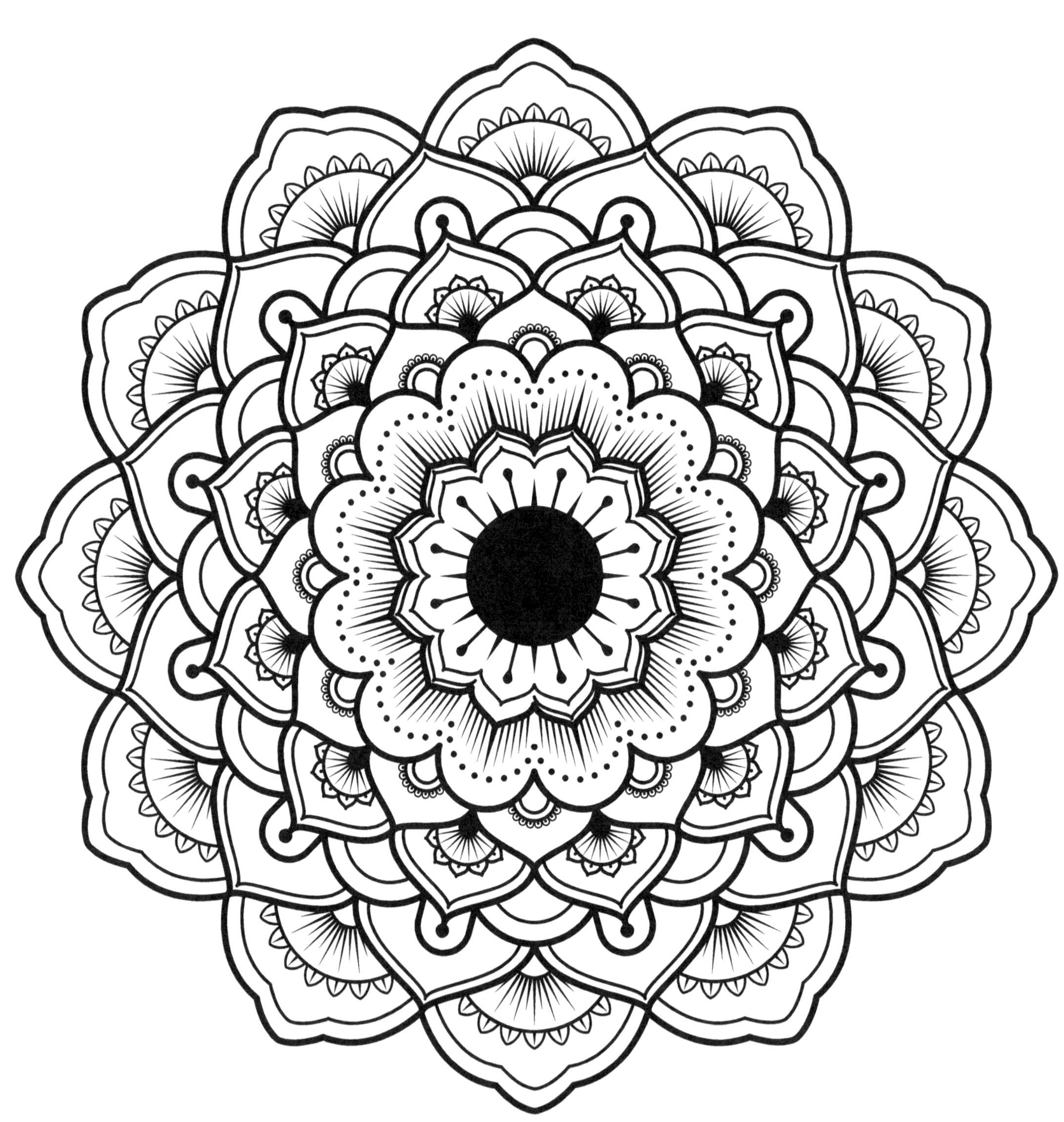

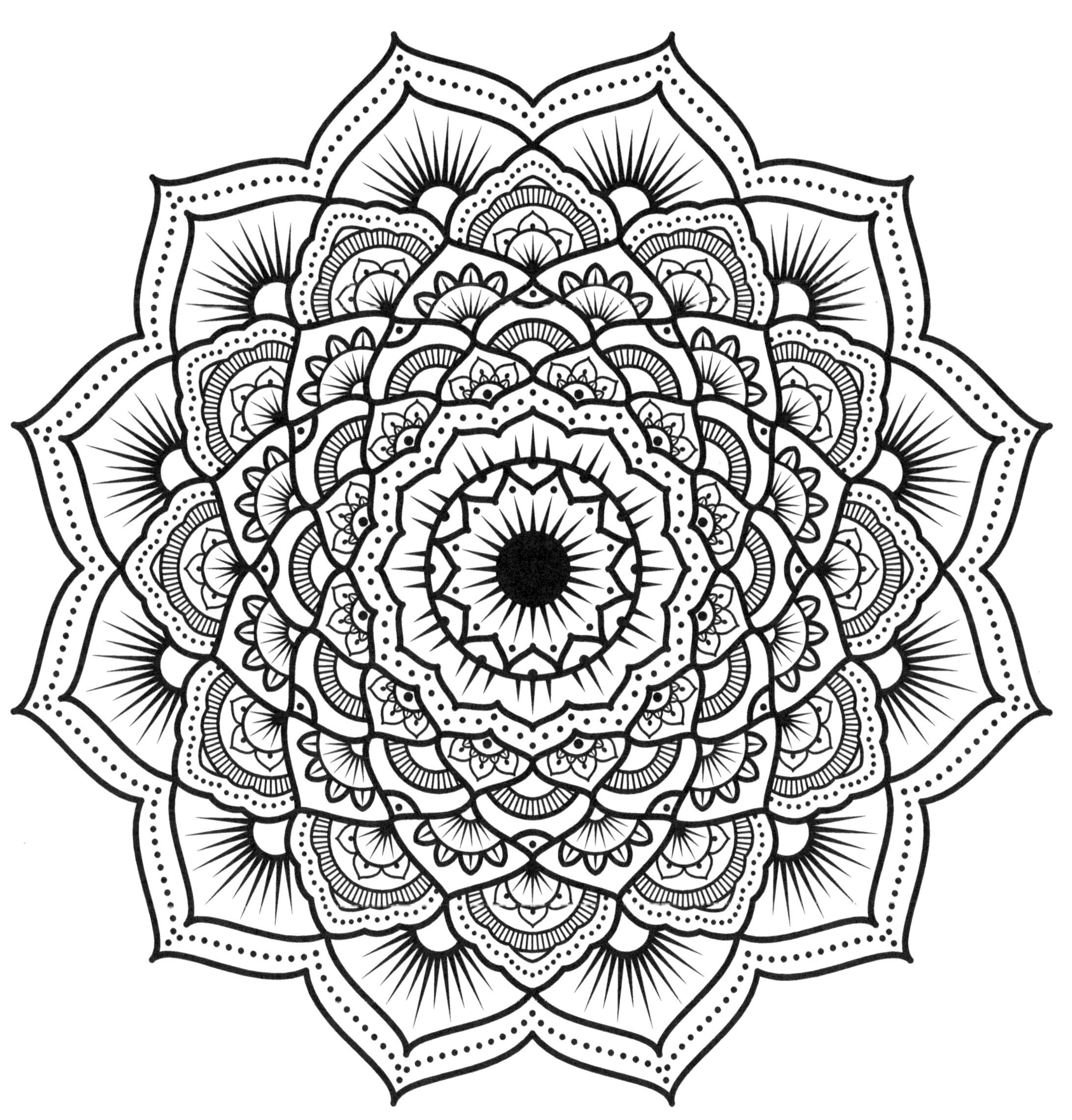

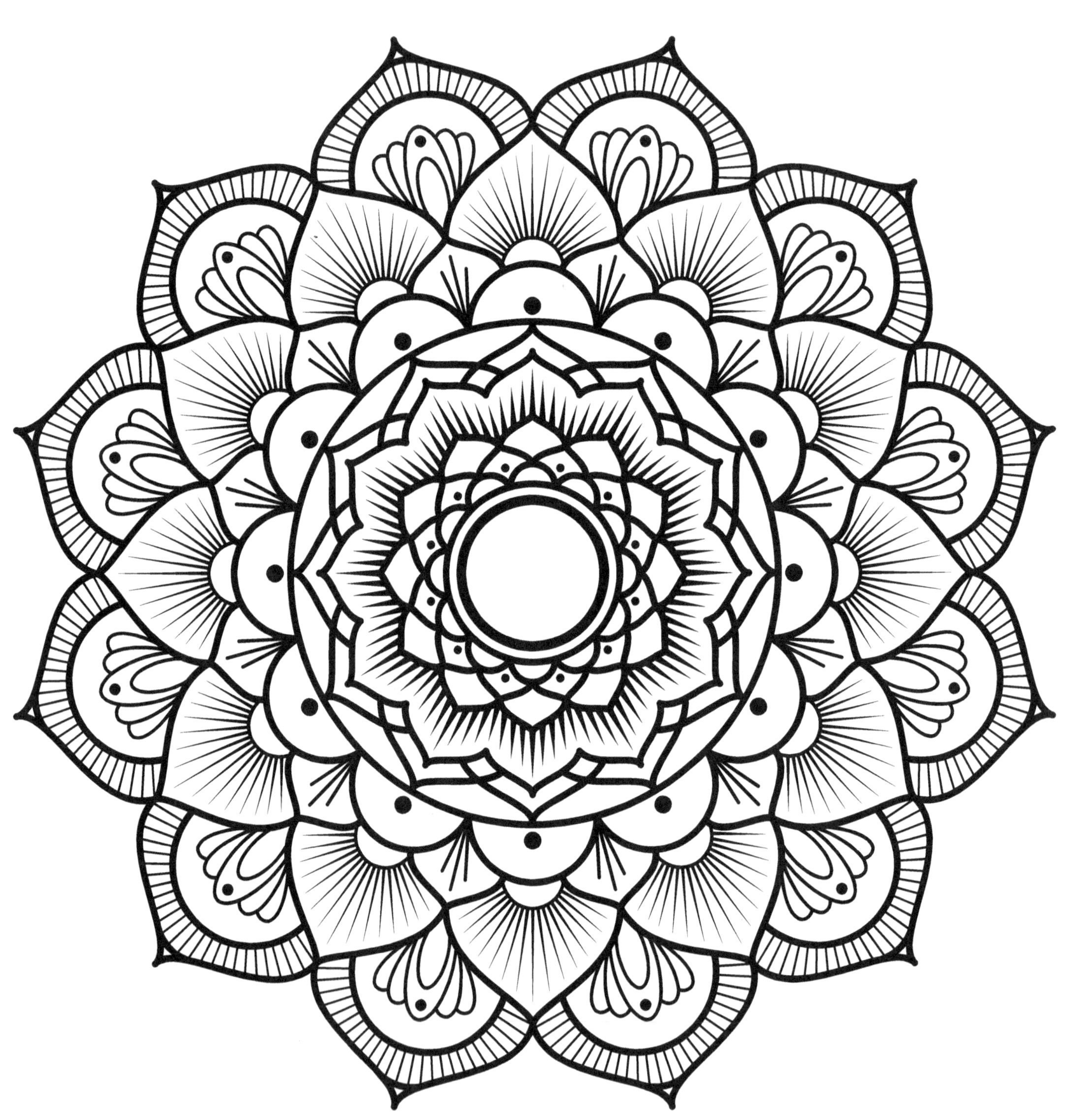

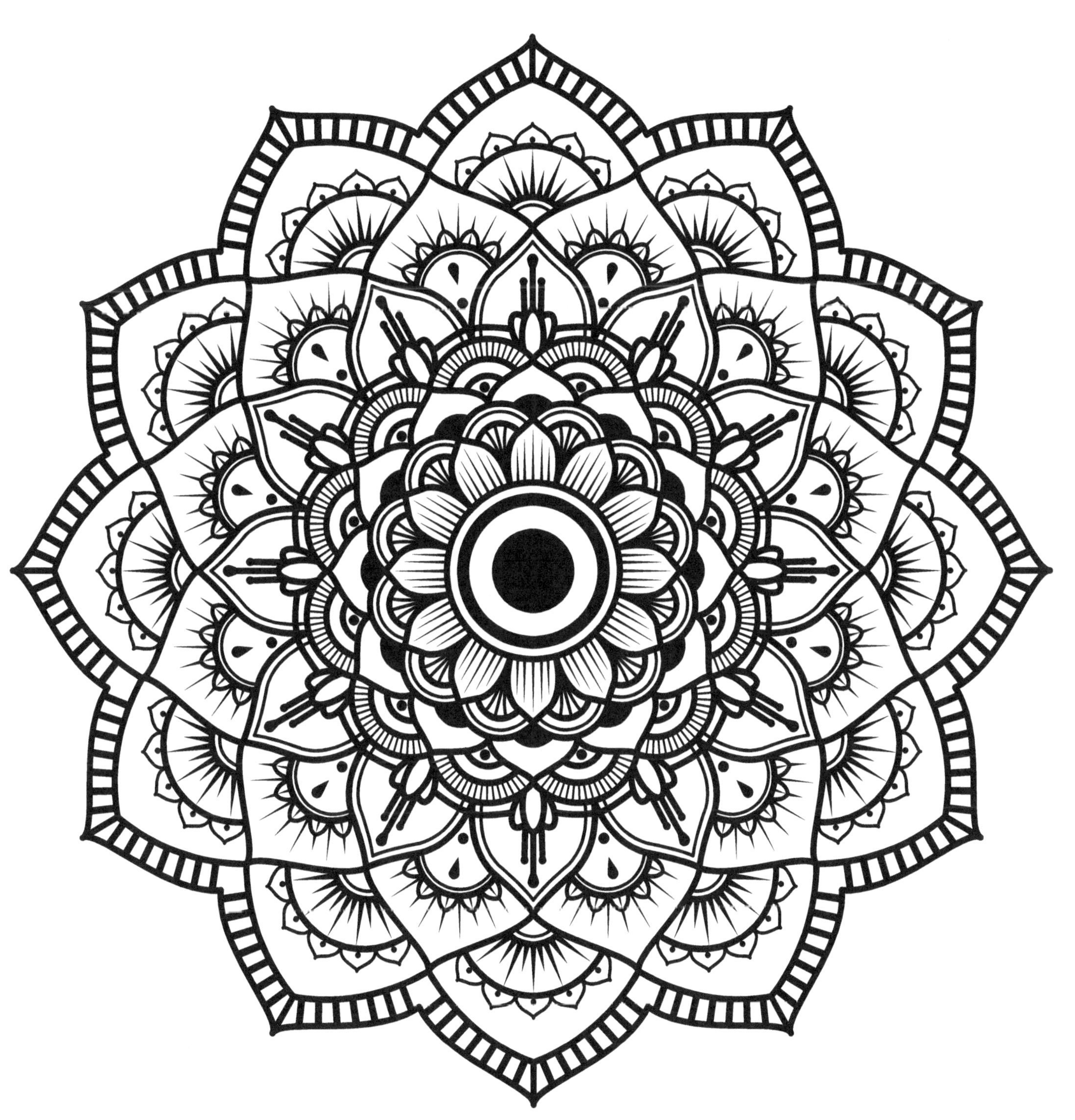

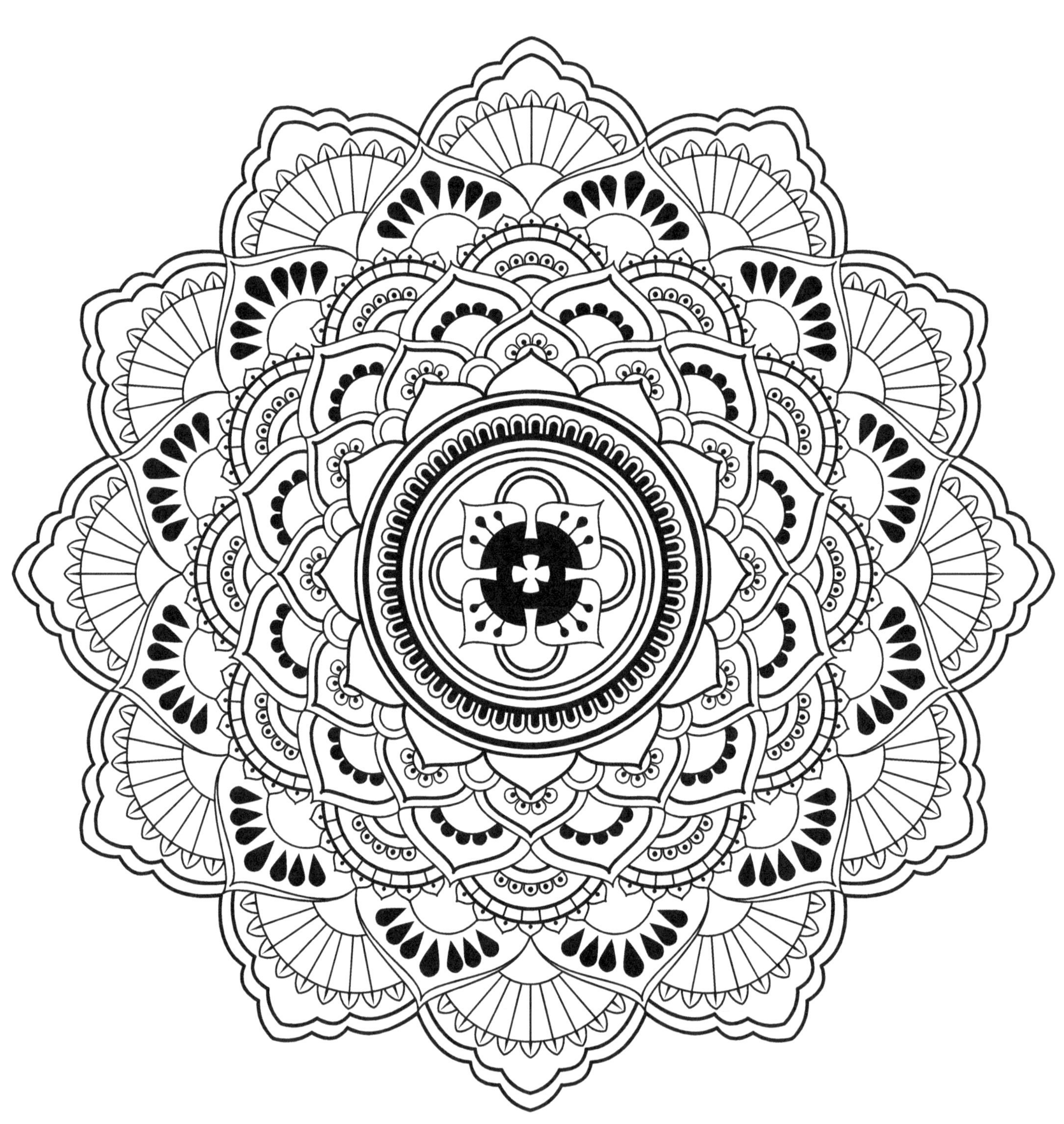

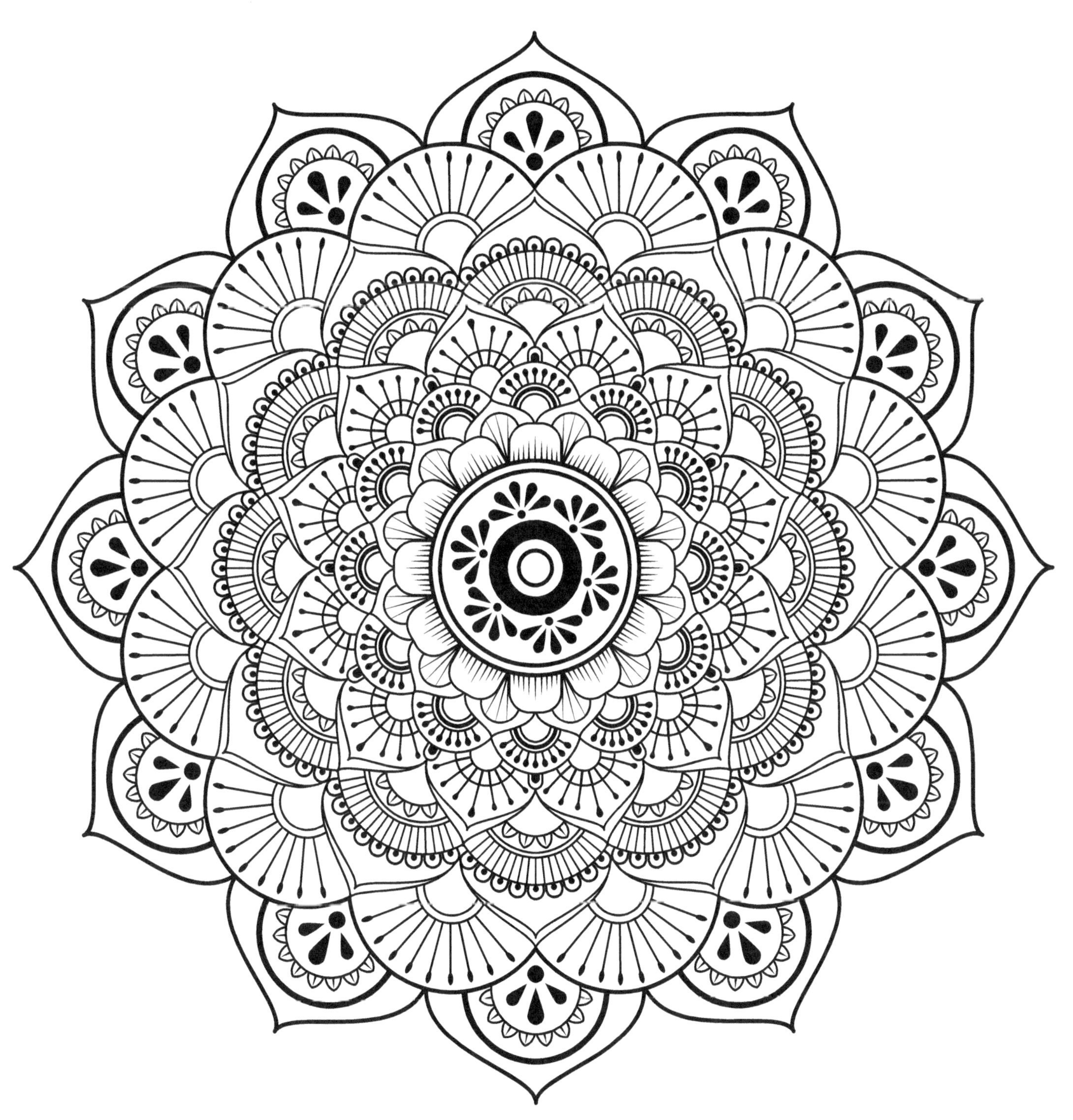

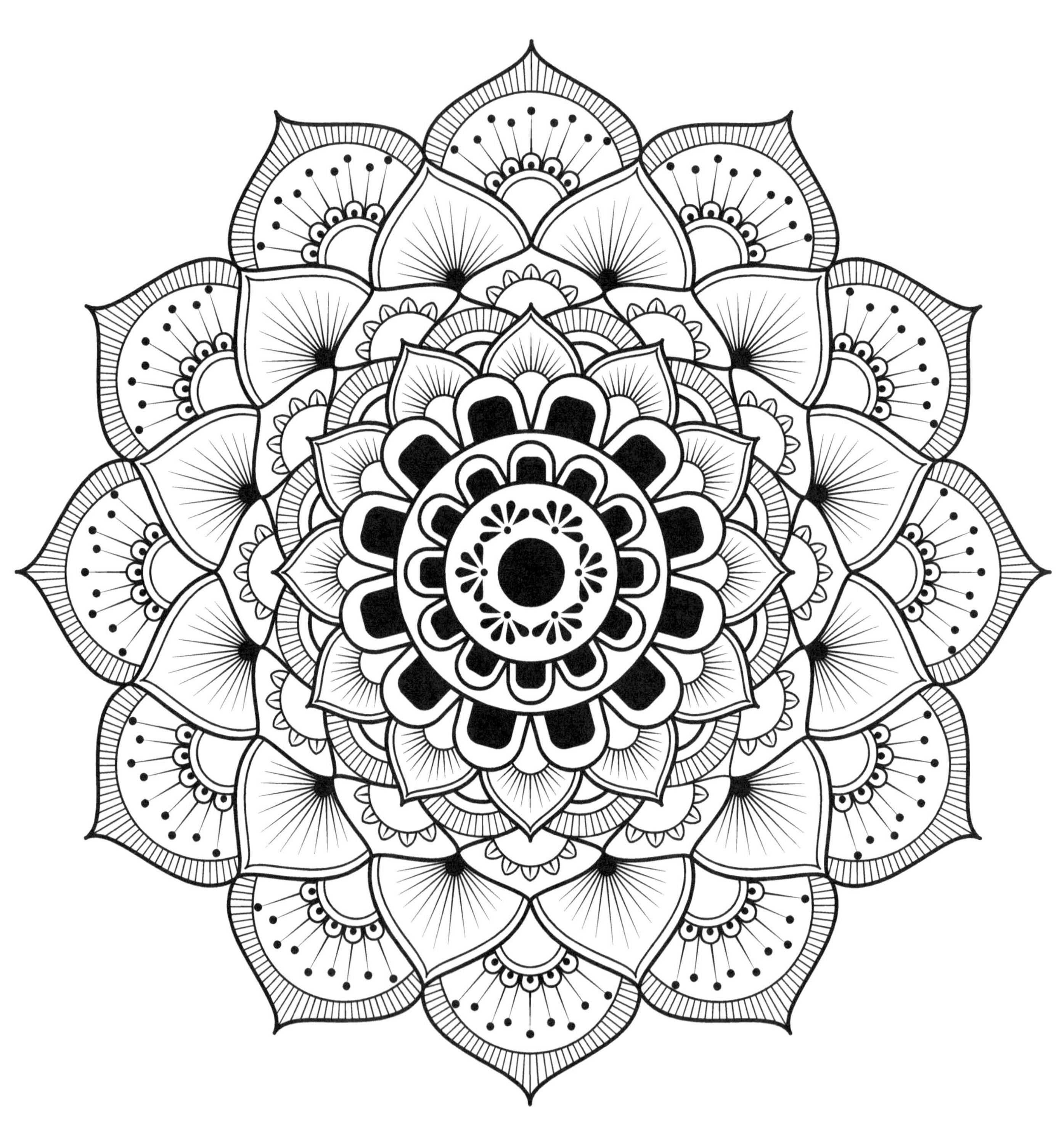

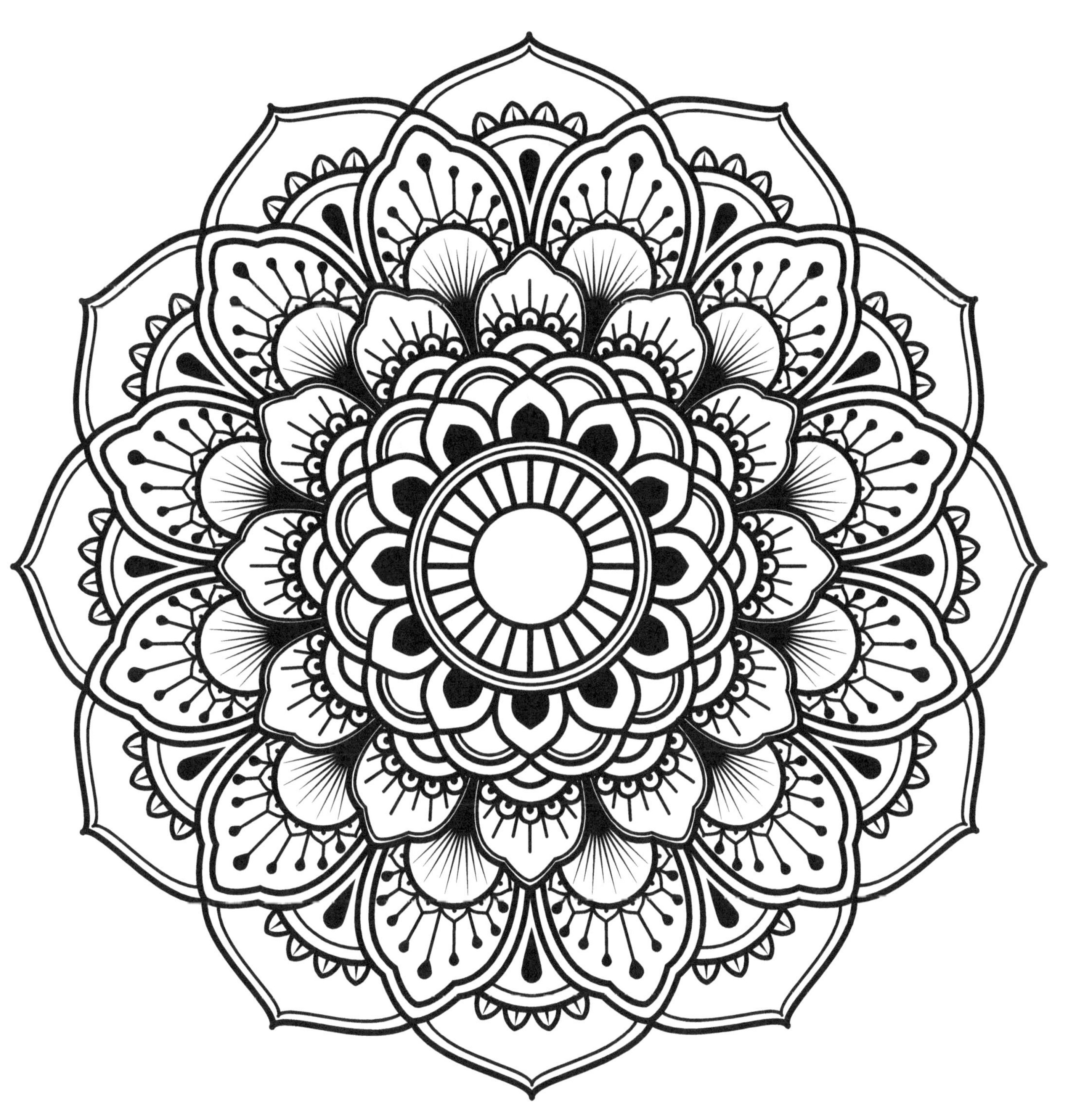

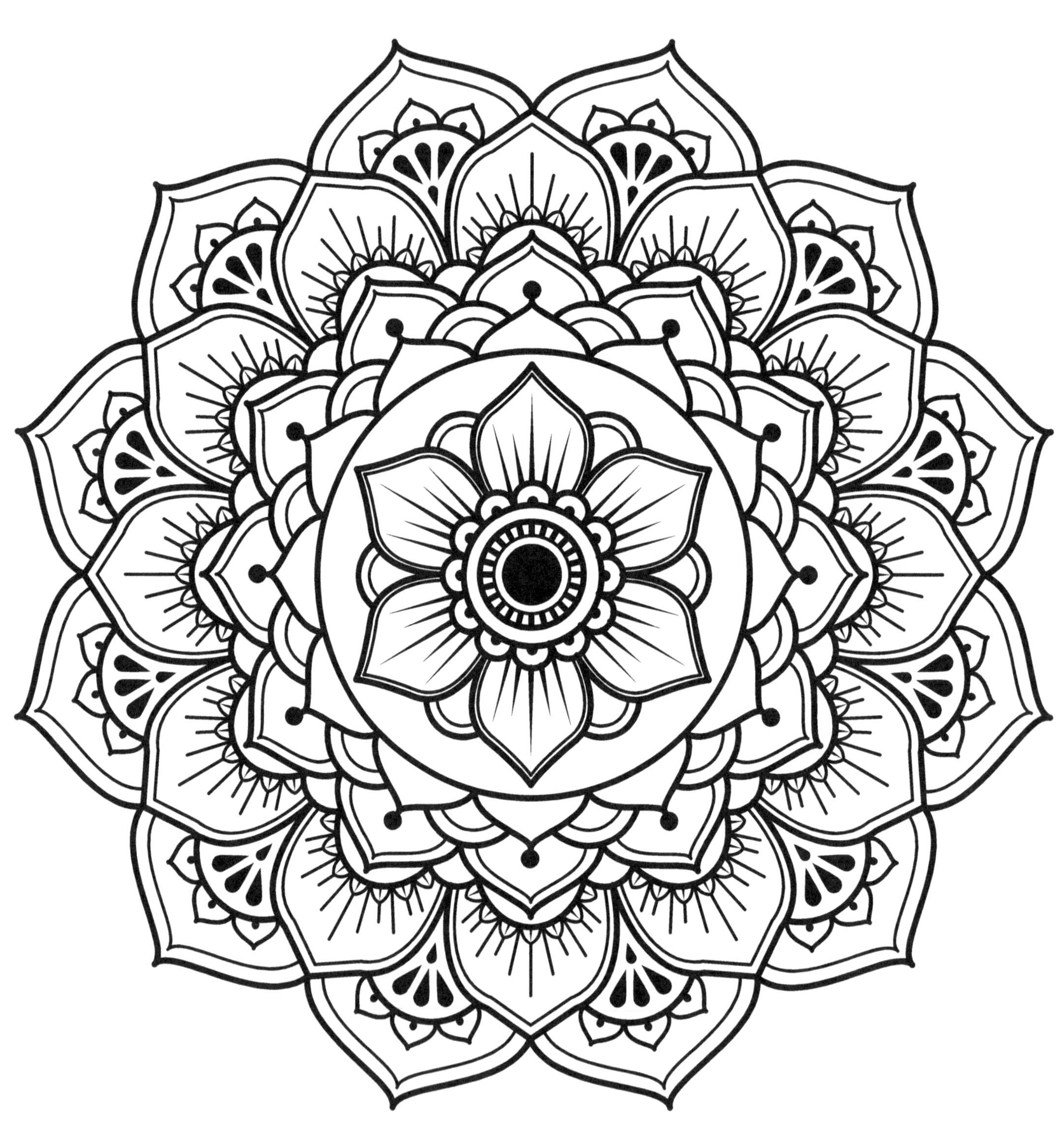

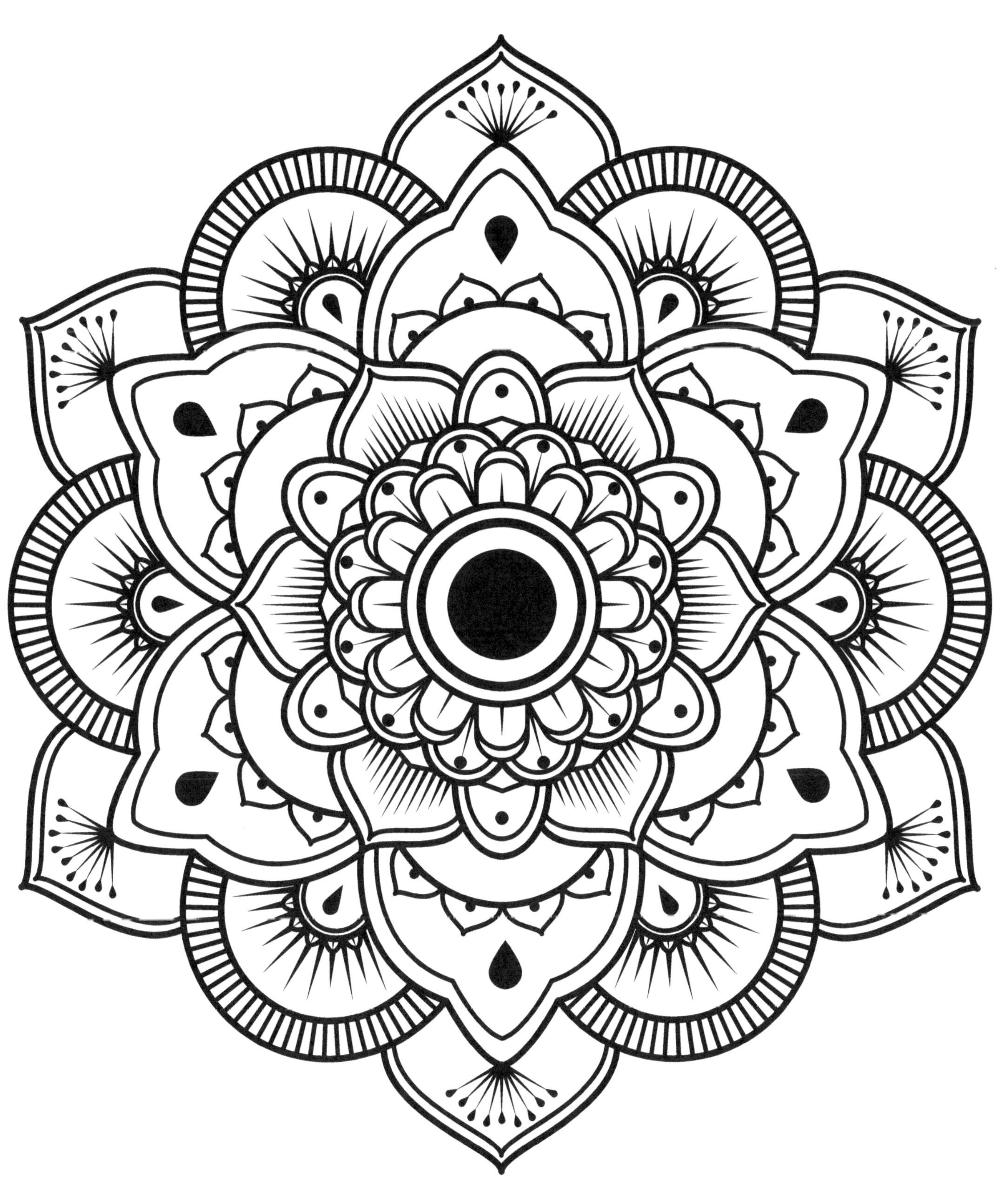

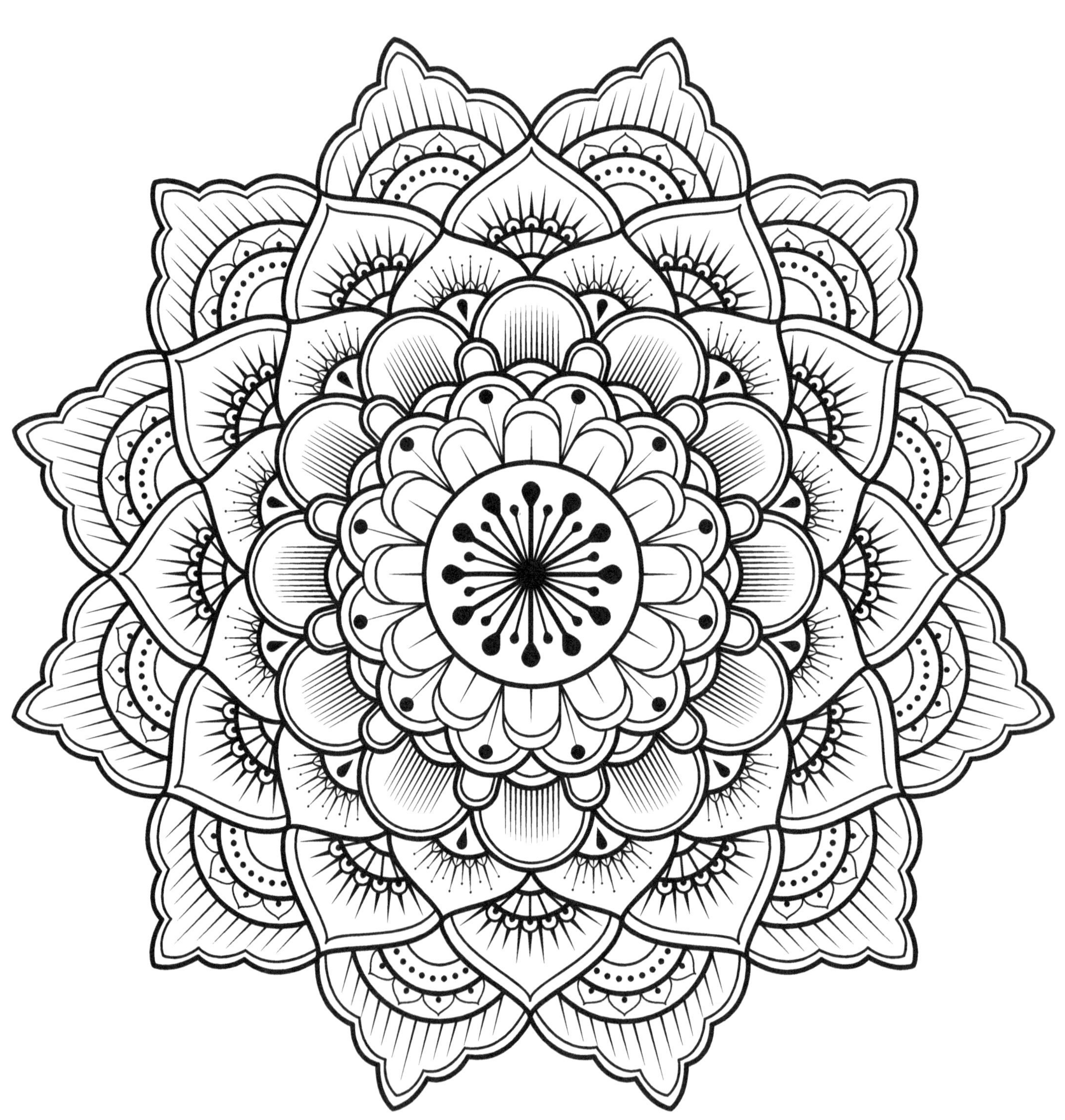

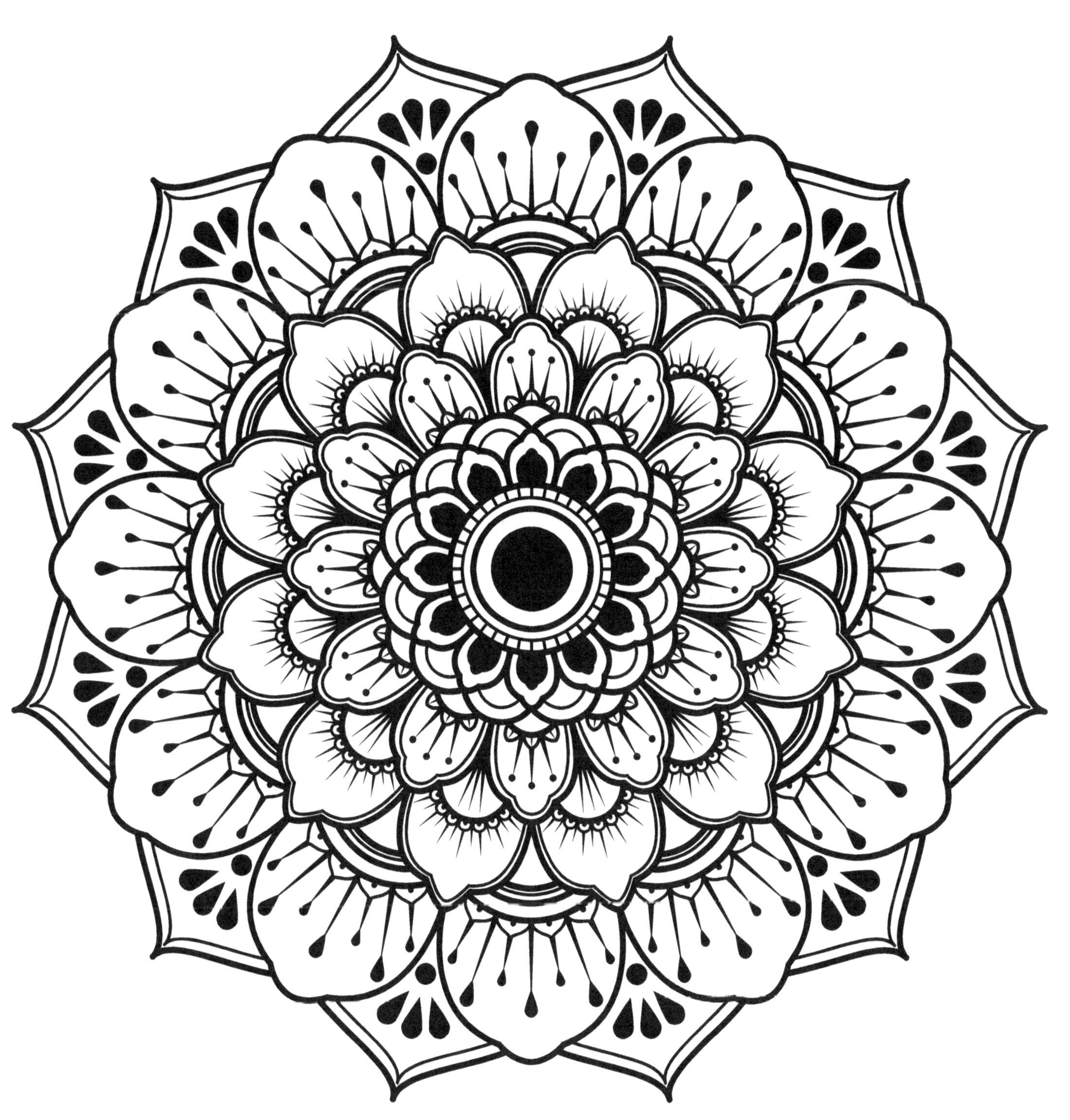

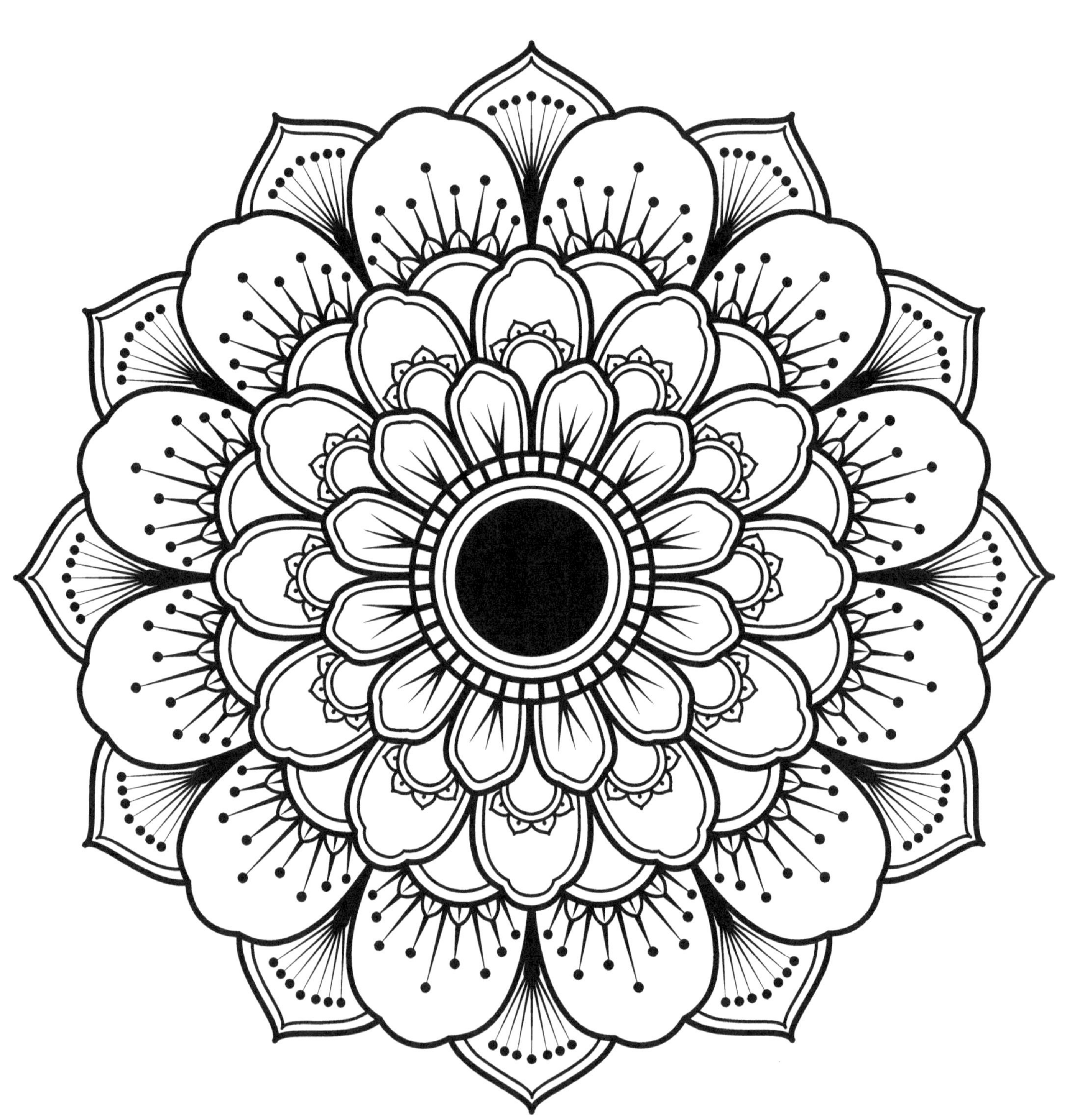

www.ingramcontent.com/pod-product-compliance
Lightning Source LLC
LaVergne TN
LVHW081254100826
845148LV00009B/1217

9781635400045